Professions
of
Faith

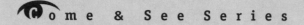

ℂome & See Series

The **Come & See Series** from Sheed & Ward is modeled on Jesus' compassionate question: "What do you seek?" and his profound invitation to "Come and see" the world through the eyes of faith (John 1:38–39). The series offers spiritual seekers lively, thought-provoking, and accessible books that explore topics of faith and the Catholic Christian tradition. Each book in the series is written by trustworthy guides who are the very best teachers, theologians, and scholars.

Series Editors: James Martin, S.J.
Jeremy Langford

Professions
of
Faith

Living and
Working
As a Catholic

edited by **James Martin, S.J.**
Jeremy Langford

SHEED & WARD
Franklin, Wisconsin
Chicago

As an apostolate of the Priests of the Sacred Heart, a Catholic religious congregation, the mission of Sheed & Ward is to publish books of contemporary impact and enduring merit in Catholic Christian thought and action. The books published, however, reflect the opinions of their authors and are not meant to represent the official position of the Priests of the Sacred Heart.

2002

Sheed & Ward
7373 South Lovers Lane Road
Franklin, Wisconsin 53132
1-800-266-5564
www.sheedandward.com

Printed in the United States of America

Cover and interior design: Biner Design and GrafixStudio, Inc.

Library of Congress Cataloging-in-Publication Data

Professions of faith : living and working as a Catholic / edited by James Martin and Jeremy Langford.
     p. cm. — (Come & see series)
  ISBN 1-58051-115-5
   1. Work—Religious aspects—Catholic Church. 2. Christian life—
   Catholic authors. 3. Vocation—Catholic Church. 4. Catholic Church—
   Doctrines. I. Martin, James, S.J. II. Langford, Jeremy. III. Come & see.
  BX1795.W67 .P76 2002
  248.4'82—dc21   2002020775

1 2 3 4 5 / 05 04 03 02

Contents

Pray as if everything depended on God;
work as if everything depended on you
—*Saint Ignatius of Loyola, 1491–1556*

Introduction

The connection between faith and work is nothing new. The women and men of the Old Testament sought to understand God's will and worked to form a deeper relationship with the Source of Life, even as, like Abraham, they questioned and, like Job, struggled. And the people of the New Testament relied on their faith as they tilled fields, fished the waters, traded their goods, and raised their families in a secular society while trying to follow the risen Christ and help build the Kingdom of God on earth.

Even though over the centuries there has been a temptation to divorce faith from work, the good news is that today there is a strong desire not only to reintegrate faith, spirituality, work, and life but also to recover the witness and wisdom of the Scriptures and tradition regarding work. There is, therefore, a healthy and natural connection between work and Christian spirituality. And one often overlooked fact is beginning to reinvigorate and transform how we learn from and live out our heritage: Jesus of Nazareth worked.

While we know practically nothing about the "hidden life" of Jesus, that is, his life between the ages of twelve and thirty, we know that he worked as a craftsman in Nazareth. (While the Greek word *technon* used by Mark and Matthew in their gospels can be translated as "craftsman" or "builder," it is traditionally rendered as "carpenter.") As a result, without too much effort we can envision Jesus being instructed by Saint Joseph, the master carpenter.

In Joseph's busy workshop in Nazareth, Jesus would probably have learned about the raw materials for his craft: which wood was best suited for chairs and tables; which worked best for yokes, for ploughs. An experienced carpenter like Joseph would have taught his young apprentice the right way to drive a nail with a hammer, the best way to hang a door, the proper way to drill a clean and deep hole in a plank, the correct way to level a ledge or lintel.

Moreover, Joseph would likely have passed on to Jesus the values necessary to become a good carpenter. You need patience (for waiting until your wood is dry and ready), judgment (for ensuring that your plumb line is straight), honesty (for charging people a fair price) and persistence (for sanding until the tabletop is smooth and clean). Alongside his teacher, a young Jesus labored and built, contributing all the while to the common good of Nazareth and the surrounding towns. And is it too difficult to imagine that the skills Jesus had learned from his teacher—patience, judgment, honesty, and persistence—would serve him well in his later ministry? In a way, the work that Jesus did in the carpentry shop helped to prepare him for his great work of spreading the good news.

Jesus worked. So did Joseph. So, of course, did Mary. And so did countless saints and holy and everyday women and men. Their faith influenced their labor—what they did for a living, what decisions they made, how they treated co-workers and customers. At the same time, their experience of work influenced and informed their faith—how they understood God's call to live whole, healthy, and happy lives in the light of gospel values.

You may have wondered why it is, then, that contemporary believers sometimes overlook the holiness of work or feel faith has nothing to say to our seemingly secular lives. Or why it is commonplace to consider work as something *separate* from our lives as Christians. Where the ancient Benedictine tradition speaks of the balance of *ora et labora* (prayer and work), the temptation today is to keep the two far apart.

Professions of Faith, the latest in Sheed & Ward's Come and See series, brings to light the interplay of faith and work in the Catholic tradition through the voices and experiences of people working in the "real world." Each contributor, an active and enthusiastic member of his or her profession, is also an active and enthusiastic Catholic. And each was asked to answer the following two questions: First, how does your faith influence your work? Second, how does your work influence your faith?

Perhaps not surprisingly, each essayist, as you'll see, takes a slightly different approach to the question of how to live out one's faith life in the workplace. Some discuss the challenges inherent in their lives at work—what is it like, for example, to be a Christian businessperson or lawyer in a highly competitive and often ethically challenging world? Or to be a police officer in a violent culture? Others discuss the quiet joys of experiencing the presence of the divine in their working lives—what is it like to deliver a baby or accompany an ill person as a Christian doctor? To be a Christian spouse, parent, architect, teacher? To create beauty as an artist? To forego higher salaries to be a social worker, to be a credible Christian journalist in a secular newsroom?

While each contributor adopts a different approach, each talks honestly and openly about the intersection of faith and work—including the struggles—in their specific situation while also striving to make their points more universal. For example, a doctor might enjoy reading about the life of a Catholic writer. Or an architect could enjoy reading about the challenges of the school teacher. But, you don't have to be a member of any of the professions represented in this book to appreciate the essays. For, in the end, every writer addresses the more basic question of what it is like to lead a life of faith in the modern world: each essay, in its own way, is relevant for all of us, no matter who we are or how we earn our daily bread.

If you read between the lines a bit, you'll also notice that the concept of "vocation" looms large in the experiences of the essayists. Even if the writers don't use the word explicitly, each essay conveys a powerful sense of *vocation*. The contributors all seem to feel, in one way or another, "called" to the type of work that they are doing. (And that's the root meaning of "vocation": it comes from the Latin verb *vocare*, meaning "to call.")

In the past, the concept of vocation was more or less reserved for priests, nuns, and brothers. "Hearing the call" usually referred to finding oneself drawn to ordination or to life in a religious community. The call was seen as almost a "mystical" event, far removed from the experience of the regular crowd of people. And this call was seen as somehow "better" or "more perfect" than the call to single or married life. Indeed, a now infamous drawing from an old catechism shows two states of life. On the left, underneath a drawing of a married couple, the legend reads: "Good." On the right, underneath a drawing of a priest celebrating Mass and a sister teaching in a classroom, the legend reads: "Better."

These days, however, the concept of vocation has rightly been seen as applying to everyone. After all, why wouldn't God call everyone in his or her own way to contribute to the building up of the Kingdom? And, as for "hearing the call," it need not be anything more mystical than enjoying your job and feeling that you're in the right place. Or, if you're not enjoying your job, it could be the feeling that you are called to be there anyway, as a sort of "leaven" at work. These are just two ways of thinking about both vocation and finding God at work. As the contributors in this volume help us understand, the key point is that your everyday work can be an integral part of your life as a Catholic.

This, incidentally, is one of the reasons that we chose not to include in the collection the quite-obvious Catholic "professions" of priest, deacon, sister, and brother. We felt that there already was plenty written about these types of vocations and, to right the balance, we would concentrate instead on types of professions that readers may not be accustomed to thinking about in terms of faith.

Overall, we hope that these essays will help you more readily to find God in your work, will encourage you to reflect on the ways that your work can inform your faith and, more broadly, will assist you in the wonderful "work" of being a Catholic in the modern world.

James Martin, S.J.
Jeremy Langford

January 24, 2002
Feast of St. Francis de Sales

Chapter 1

Hotly in Pursuit of the Real: On Being a Catholic Writer

Ron Hansen

Ever since I learned to read, I have wanted to be a fiction writer. The vocation was inchoate at first, for books seem as authorless as rain to a child, but it insisted that I not only inhabit the world imagined by others, as good readers do, but go on with the story, configure it to fit my own life, filch it like candy left out in a bowl. Robert Coles has named this odd hankering and delight "the call of stories."

I may have been five or so when I first noticed that calling. At Sunday Mass in Omaha, Nebraska, the priest ascended the stairs to the high pulpit at Holy Angels Church, announced a reading from one of the gospels, and after a few sentences of the passage, I suddenly was aware that the story was familiar to me. Say it was the shockingly concrete scene in Mark where Jesus heals a blind man by wetting the man's eyes with his spittle. I found myself anticipating the next moves, certain the man would say he could see people but that they looked like trees walking. And Jesus would lay his hands on the afflicted man's eyes again, and then the man would see everything clearly. The sentences were sure and predictable to me; I felt I was finally their audience; and I realized with a good deal of wonder that the gospels were like those children's books that my mother or sisters would read to me over and over again. With great seriousness, the priest would read aloud the same stunning stories from the life of Christ, and, when he was finished reading, he would talk intelligently about the meaning of the passage in our own lives, and even the old in the congregation would watch and listen like children being taught.

The liturgical rites were grand theater then, filled with magisterial ceremony, great varieties of mystery and symbol, and a haunting Gregorian chant that sounded lovely even if poorly sung. And since I could not yet follow the English translation of the priest's Latin in my missal, I would fix my gaze high overhead on the soft blue sky of the dome on which there was a huge, literal, and beautiful painting of Christ being escorted by the holy angels on his ascension to Heaven, his loose white clothing floating off him so that most of his flesh was exposed.

Looking back on my childhood now, I find that church-going and religion were in good part the origin of my vocation as a writer, for along with Catholicism's feast for the senses, its ethical concerns, its insistence on seeing God in all things, and the high status it gave to Scripture, drama, and art, there was a connotation in Catholicism's liturgies that storytelling mattered. Each Mass was a narrative steeped in meaning and metaphor, helping the faithful to not only remember the past but to make it present here and now, and to bind ourselves into a sharing group so that, ideally, we could continue the public ministry of Jesus in our world.

On the other hand, my vocation as a writer was also called forth by something unnamable that I can only associate with a yen to live out, in my imagination, other lives and possibilities, a craving that eventually made acting attractive to my brother Rob and soon made storytelling necessary to me.

In kindergarten, for example, we had an afternoon period of show-and-tell. A few minutes earlier a boy named Kenneth breathlessly told me about the side altar at some European cathedral his family had visited, where a pressure-sensitive *prie-dieu* illuminated a crucifix when penitents fell on their knees there to pray. Seeing my fascination, the five-year-old went further, confusing the scene and himself with flashing colors and whirling mechanisms that seemed lifted from a science-fiction movie. I fell into my own imagination as Sister Martha went from child to child, asking them to report on adventures, discoveries, encounters, or anything else they thought noteworthy. And then she got to me. And I instinctively said a neighbor had turned a hallway closet into a chapel, with holy pictures everywhere, and there were lots of candles burning all the time, because that was the only light, and there was a kneeler in front of a crucifix and when you knelt on it real blood trickled out of the wounds in Christ's hands and feet. Real blood? Sister Martha asked. Well, it looked like real blood, it was red like blood, and it trickled down his face from the crown of thorns, too. She squinted at me with just a twitch of a smile, and I was shocked, even insulted, that she could think I was making this up. Hadn't I seen that hallway closet, that padded *prie-dieu*, that crucifix with my own eyes? I could describe the finest detail, I could smell the candle wax as it burned. Stifling her amusement, the kindergarten teacher questioned me more closely, possibly having found a kids-say-the-darndest-things instance that she could present like a chocolate pie to her sisters at dinner, and I just kept embellishing and filling in gaps in the narrative until Sister Martha seemed to decide I was depleted and she shifted to another child. And when I looked at Kenneth, he was wide-eyed and in awe, with no hint of affront for my having stolen his show-and-tell, but with a certain amount of jealousy that I'd seen a *prie-dieu* that was far superior to his and, worse, seemed to have tried to selfishly keep it to myself.

Within the year I would be reading on my own and finding out about children's books and children's authors and their need to do just what I did: to alter the facts that seemed imposed and arbitrary, to intensify scenes and situations with additions and falsifications, and to ameliorate the dull and slack commodities of experience with the zest of the wildest imaginings.

The first author whose name I remembered and whose stories I hunted down was Jules Verne, whom I avidly read in third grade. In fourth grade it was Albert Payson Terhune—I even named our foundling pup after his "Lad"—and *Peck's Bad Boy* by Aurand Harris, with its gladdening irony that a boy who was continually getting into trouble with grownups might simply be just acting like boys do. Then it was fifth grade and the Hardy Boys and Tom Swift, books meant for kids my age but which seemed hopelessly old-fashioned and did not thrill me nearly so much as the tales of Edgar Allan Poe, who so hooked me that I held his book of horror stories open in my lap to sneak peeks at as I pretended to take classroom notes. I was drawing and painting then, not writing fiction. A friend's father was an illustrator and I fantasized that I would have a job like that when I got out of school. But gradually an urgency to write fiction took over; it was a vocation that seemed so exalted and sacred and beyond me that I would not even talk about it.

In "Confessions of a Reluctant Catholic," novelist Alice McDermott recalls learning to be a writer, which "seemed to me from the outset to be an impossible pursuit, one for which I had no preparation or training, or even motive, except for a secret and undeniable urge to do so." She'd discovered that "fiction made the chaos bearable, fiction transformed the absurdity of our brief lives by giving context and purpose and significance to every gesture, every desire, every detail. Fiction transformed the meaningless, fleeting stuff of daily life into the necessary components of an enduring work of art."[1]

The intuition of the fiction writer is similar to that of the scientist, that the world is governed by rules and patterns that are, by analysis and experiment, detectable, that the hidden mysteries of nature can be interrogated and solved. I have run into people who don't read fiction because they feel it's founded on fabrications and swindles and worthless extenuations of reality—a famous professional golfer once complained about English classes in college where he was forced to read "these big, fat books that weren't even true"—but for many of us fiction holds up to the light, fathoms, simplifies, and refines those existential truths that, without such interpretation, seem all too secret, partial, and elusive. And that, of course, is the goal of religion as well.

Some writers are agnostic and have as their religion art, but just as many are conscious that the source of their gifts is God and have found thanksgiving, worship, and praise of the Holy Being to be central to their lives and artistic practices. In *An American Requiem: God, My Father, and the War that Came Between Us*, James Carroll wrote that, "The very act of storytelling, of arranging memory and invention according to the structure of narrative is, by definition, holy."[2] And in a later interview, Carroll stated that "my notion of narrative informs my faith, and my notion of faith informs my idea of what writing is for."

Writing not only gives form and meaning to our sometimes disorderly existence, but gives the author the chance for self-disclosure and communion with others, while giving readers a privileged share in another's inner life that, perhaps imperceptibly, questions and illuminates their own. Reading attentively, connecting our lives with those of fictional characters, choosing ethically and emotionally just as they do or in contradistinction to them, we enter the realm of the spirit where we simultaneously discover our likeness to others and our difference, our uniqueness. Questioning ourselves and our world, finding in it, for all its coincidence, accidents, and contingencies, a mysterious coherence, we may become aware of a horizon beyond which abides the One who is the creator and context of our existence.

Writing on the Catholic short-story master Andre Dubus, Tobias Wolff noted that in his friend's work, "the quotidian and the spiritual don't exist on different planes, but infuse each other. His is an unapologetically sacramental vision of life in which ordinary things participate in the miraculous, the miraculous in ordinary things. He believes in God, and talks to him, and doesn't mince words . . . He is open to mystery, and of all mysteries, the one that interests him most is the human potential for transcendence."[3]

Edifying Christian fiction can have a tendency to attenuate the scandal of the incarnation by circumscribing the sensual or sordid facts of the flesh in order to concentrate on heavenly actions and aspirations. And in doing so, such fiction fails both the mysteries we are informed of by faith and those mysteries of sin and redemption we perceive in our daily lives. We need Christian fiction writers who are, in Flannery O'Connor's phrase, "hotly in pursuit of the real." She noted that "the chief difference between the novelist who is an orthodox Christian and the novelist who is merely a naturalist is that the Christian novelist lives in a larger universe.

He believes that the natural world contains the supernatural. And this doesn't mean that his obligation to portray nature is less; it means it is greater."[4]

In an essay entitled "How to Be an American Novelist in Spite of Being Southern and Catholic," Walker Percy identified the inherent congeniality of Christianity to the vocation of the novelist. "The Christian ethos," he wrote,

> sustains the narrative enterprise in ways so familiar to us that they can be overlooked. It underwrites those very properties of the novel without which there is no novel; I am speaking of the mystery of human life, its sense of predicament, of something having gone wrong, of life as a wayfaring and a pilgrimage, of the density and linearity of time and the sacramental reality of things. The intervention of God in history through the Incarnation bestows a weight and value to the individual human narrative which is like money in the bank to the novelist. Original Sin is out of fashion, both with Christians and with Jews, let alone unbelievers. But any novelist who does not believe that his character finds himself in a predicament not entirely of his own making or of society's making is in trouble as a novelist. And any novelist who begins his novel with his character in a . . . predicament which is a profound mystery to which

> he devotes his entire life to unraveling . . . is a closet
> Jew or Christian whether he likes it or not.[5]

Even in high school it was my habit to send off my short stories to magazines for possible publication. I was never very disappointed when they were rejected, for I had no illusions that my callow stories were any good, but I had never in my life met a fiction writer, and the profession seemed so magnificent to me that my quest to try it seemed outlandish. My regular submissions to magazines were messages in a bottle, ways of keeping contact with a lovesick yearning that was gradually becoming my soul's signature. And then when I was a junior at Creighton, a short story that was the first I felt proud of was rejected by the *Atlantic Monthly* with a letter from the fiction editor gently indicating the errors and holes in that particular story, while generously urging me to send in something else.

I ought to have been gladdened by that letter, but instead I was dejected, because in spite of the fiction editor's notes to me, the necessary skills and discipline of revision were not yet mine, and I hadn't the slightest notion of how to make my flawed and unfinished story any better than it was. And I found myself wondering if I wasn't kidding myself about my talent and wasting my time in a foolish and vainglorious pursuit.

And then a picture flashed in my mind for just a fraction of a second. It was there—and then, instantly, it was not. But I was sure that God had favored me with a foretaste of the future, for what I fleetingly glimpsed was a page in a magazine like *Time* or *Newsweek* and a few inches of a column that was indisputably a book review. I couldn't read the book's title or any other words on that page, but I knew with rock-hard intensity that the book being reviewed was by me. With that one look, major questions were answered, a critical juncture, perhaps, was passed, and I was flooded with feelings of calm and bliss and purposefulness.

Writing on vocation in *Magister Ludi*, the great German novelist Herman Hesse noted, "There are many types and kinds of call, but the core of the experience is always the same: your soul is awakened, transformed, or exalted, so that instead of dreams and presentiments from within, a summons comes from without, a portion of reality presents itself and makes a claim."

I have discovered in late night conversations that many of my friends have had profound experiences of God's hand, God's voice, God's solace, God's gentle invitation. But how often are those experiences written about? And yet they are as important, indelible, and real as anything else that happens to us. Catholic writers may principally differ from others in their heightened awareness of the unseen but ineluctable foundation of our existence, and in their unsqueamish and unembarrassed insistence that one is hotly in pursuit of the real especially when writing about the substance of things hoped for.

Questions for Reflection: *The role of a writer is to highlight key aspects of life and experience that might otherwise be missed. What makes a* Catholic *writer distinctive? What might it mean to be "hotly in pursuit of the real"? What would you say is a "sacramental vision" of life? Why are stories important to the life of faith? In what ways does the work of storytelling nourish faith and the work of faith nourish fiction? How is the Mass a story?*

Notes

1. Alice McDermott, "Confessions of a Reluctant Catholic," *Commonweal* (February 11, 2000).

2. James Carroll, *An American Requiem: God, My Father, and the War that Came Between Us* (Boston: Houghton Mifflin, 1996).

3. Andre Dubus, *Broken Vessels*, with an introduction by Tobias Wolff (Boston: David R. Godine, Publisher, 1991), xv.

4. Flannery O'Connor, *Mystery and Manners*, selected and edited by Sally and Robert Fitzgerald (New York: Farrar, Straus & Giroux, 1961), 175.

5. Walker Percy, *Signposts in a Strange Land*, ed. Patrick Samway, S.J. (New York: Farrar, Straus & Giroux), 178.

Chapter 2

Building on a Firm Foundation: On Being a Catholic Businessperson

Lucie J. Fjeldstad

I have been in the computer industry for thirty-five years, thirty of those in management. My Catholic upbringing in rural California was enhanced by valuable time spent at Santa Clara University. My effectiveness to weave my Catholic upbringing into the workplace and then to incorporate appropriate reflections in my family life is probably best exemplified by the years I have most recently spent working with a start-up computer software company. This company had about twenty-five employees when I was asked by one of the company's board of directors to provide some guidance to the founders. The lead founder was then the CEO.

To look at the company at that time, it was a collection of technologists, an accountant, a salesperson, and the founders. There were no company policies, including no guidelines as to how the company would operate, and no policies for hiring or taking care of the employees. The founders included a young entrepreneur (the CEO) whose biggest asset was his ability to see the future of the industry; his biggest shortcoming was his inability to face his own weaknesses. He had successfully built and sold a company very quickly, without learning any of the lessons that a mature business teaches its executives. As I saw it, he had not learned how to listen or to value his team, and he did not possess the skills to build the right foundation for the company—bringing long-term value to its employees and shareholders. The other founder was an engineer who was an easy-going person but had little management experience. He was thought to be an excellent software developer. As for the other employees, most were very young and inexperienced. They had not been working long enough to understand the value of a sense of loyalty. The culture of the high-tech industry (before the demise of the dot-com companies) was that job shopping and making a quick dollar were prevalent throughout the area.

After evaluating the company, I told the board that what this company needed was a mother, a mentor, a leader, and a sense of soul—not necessarily in that order. In truth, I never thought of myself as being a role model for embodying all of these characteristics. Valuing people and operating with integrity had been such fundamental principles in my life; I never gave them a second thought. The board asked me to work with the CEO to begin the process of "growing" the company and establishing a foundation for success. So, it was now time consciously to put these principles to work.

We concluded that we needed to do three things: (1) establish a value system; (2) "clean house," which meant "firing and hiring" as appropriate; and (3) instill teamwork. As we began taking these actions, it became apparent that the role of advisor for me was inadequate for the task at hand. The longer I was with the company, the more dependent the CEO became on me. As we thought about the reasons for his dependency, it became obvious that he realized he needed management skills.

As time wore on, what became obvious to me was that what the business needed at this formative point was a heart and character and conscience. After long discussions and soul-searching sessions, we concluded that the founders' abrupt style was not effective and did not embody the Christian approach we felt was required to create a company that people wanted to be a part of. While our employees were not Catholics, they were Christians. So, instead of bringing religious quotes, church documents, or the sacraments into the business world, I introduced and nurtured Christian values and ethics. Through these values, especially the notion of the "common good," we were well able to build a company with a soul in which everyone celebrated and worked together for the betterment of themselves and the company as a whole. This was a major realization for our founder since he had previously built a company with little concern for opinions contrary to his own, and he believed that his approach was a formula for success. Sadly, achieving what he believed to be success with his first business (that is, selling it for a phenomenal amount of money), led him to conclude his personal management style was faultless. Ultimately, he and I jointly concluded that I should take over the business; he became the advisor and I became the CEO. To this day, he believes that the decision for us to swap roles was the best thing for the company. As it turned out, the other founder, his second in command, would be our next challenge, because he "felt the sheep were there for the benefit of the shepherd." We did not realize this until the real work began.

We started with the value system. We assembled the management team and worked with them to create a core set of values, which we presented to the other employees as a "draft." We asked them to help us make the draft a better set of principles that we all would keep or commitments we would make to each other. They did a terrific job! We wrote down the values and made posters for all of the walls in the company. This was the first step in what has become an ongoing process of establishing and living by Christian business ethics. My objective was to mentor and guide the company with Jesus as my role model. To "fast forward" a bit, we can proudly say that today every employee can quickly recite the company's values and lives them each day. These tenets are

1) *Passion for customer success:* We are easy to do business with. We set priorities and think through desired outcomes and obstacles. We make informed, intelligent commitments, which we keep.

2) *Winning together:* We win by exceeding our common goals, celebrating our successes, and having fun.

3) *Innovative spirit:* We are partners in innovation, advancing the way our customers do business. We provide a fast-paced, challenging, and creative work environment that encourages and rewards risk-taking.

4) *We hire and develop the best people:* We expect and appreciate the highest level of accountability, thought, and drive from one another. We resolve our differences promptly and respectfully.

5) *Integrity:* Our actions are based upon sound moral principles: honesty, trust, and respect.

Once we created our value system, we assessed the ability of each employee to embrace and live by the values we had agreed on. Sadly, it became necessary to dismiss a few of the employees who could not live by these tenets. Unfortunately, the biggest dissenter ended up being the second founder of the company, whose personal value system, despite the façade of a Christian lifestyle, was, in my opinion, corrupt. He had prejudices and scruples that proved to be less than honorable, and he encouraged his staff to emulate his behavior. He laughed off his misbehaviors, including bragging to me that he had gotten ahead in his career by not telling the truth. But dismissing him from the business was one of the best things that ever happened to him. In the months following his departure, he appeared to have thought about his attitudes and behavior and has subsequently endeavored to reestablish acquaintances in a Christian manner with those he left behind.

The departure of one other dissenter also had a profound impact on the company. This person was our key conduit with a major customer and did an outstanding job of meeting the customers' technical requirements. Unfortunately, he had a huge chip on his shoulder and, as it turned out, had a reputation for always degrading the company and the people he worked with in the presence of others. When it became clear that he could not live by our values, we released him. Our salesperson for this particular customer was distraught over our decision. He said, "You can't let him go; we're about to get a big order, and without him on our team, we won't get it." We told the salesperson that we believed we would get the order without this person on the team because he was wrong for our team and wrong for the customer.

In the end, we got the order, we retained the customer, and the customer said it was because we practiced the values we preached. The young salesperson learned a valuable lesson: Values are more important than money, and if you stick to those values, the money may be a positive by-product.

Dismissing employees is *never* an easy thing and requires honesty, dignity, and respect. Jesus never fired anyone but then he did not inherit any disciples and he hired well.

If there is one thing I have learned in my personal Christian life it is that none of us is an island; we are all part of something greater. For me, it begins at home with my family. I carry this commitment to family to work and on to our family of customers and our community. This is the *mantra* that we, therefore, have endeavored to instill in our management team and other employees. Our family comes first. Therefore, when we celebrate as a company, we celebrate the successes we have achieved and we celebrate as a family with our families present.

We then began a regimented hiring and training process for all employees, built on the value system as the foundation, but augmented by improved communications and a training/reward/recognition process across the company. In doing so, we helped each employee find meaning and purpose in their work, instilling a conviction that each employee is as important as the other. Our motto is that we all work "with" each other; no one works "for" anyone else. We instituted last-Friday-of-the-month socials and intra-departmental sporting events on the belief that a "company who plays together stays together." We have monthly company meetings and bi-weekly company updates. Believing that the "coach" is only as good as his or her team, executives continuously walk the floors to visit with and get to know their people better. We conducted our first confidential employee opinion survey last fall to underscore the fact that we were serious about listening to and addressing employees' concerns. This was a way to confirm that we were handling their issues, and was a way to indeed make certain that we had all issues at hand. We learned many things from that first survey. It clearly pointed out how successful our ethics programs had become, but it also indicated that we needed to accelerate our "teamwork" agenda.

Teamwork was our next focus. Just as Jesus chose Paul, one of the best-educated men of his time, and Matthew, skilled in the business of the day, we chose our senior executive team based on their skills and their virtues. Each executive needed to become infused with our enthusiasm for the vision of the company, and each needed to be an evangelist of sorts, able to speak about it with frankness, fervor, and faith. Each needed to believe that there was "no *I* in the word *team*" (or, it must be all about "we" and not all about "me," as we often say) and make certain the employees conduct themselves in the same manner. Differences, and there are naturally some in a diverse business environment, need to be respected and settled respectfully. This approach has improved loyalty and has helped put employee and customer ahead of making a fast buck. There may not be "an *I* in the word *team*," but there is "an *I* in the word *jail*" in our company. And employees in our company know that the way they get in "jail" is to not conduct themselves in an ethical manner.

Being an ethical person starts with one knowing and having the courage and strength to be true to one's self. This requires a personal foundation, which includes faith, family, and/or experience. It differs for each person. For me, it comes from all three aspects. Being honest and telling the truth are employment imperatives in our company. It is refreshing to see how many employees who were with us when I first came to the company have grown to be better people and hence better employees and citizens and children of God by the careful, yet deliberate, personal instilling of this critical value.

We have completed the first phases of our action plans to build the foundation for the company. Because life in the business world is a journey, not an event, we are always looking to improve. The business has grown to over 220 employees. Employee morale has never been higher. Our customers will each speak positively to our attention to making them successful and to our value set and how we live these values. Our board is ready to take the company public at the first opportunity.

To bring the conversation back to what the relationship between faith and work has meant to me, I start with the belief that none of us is an island. We never stop learning in life. We will continue to learn new lessons on earth until we are no longer here. In the world of business, you are presented with challenges that parallel your personal life. Examples include: (1) working with people from different walks of life, with different values and perspectives; (2) balancing one's personal and professional lives; and (3) being asked to do something that you find unethical that sadly is common in the corporate business world. In each of these situations, we are provided an opportunity for self-improvement. What you learn from these situations and how you handle yourself determine the person you are. I have welcomed these challenges because I have discovered I am far more religious than I have given myself credit for.

Business pressures have given me strength. How I have reacted to these situations continually holds up a mirror to my character and conscience. I strive to be proud of what I see in that mirror. We hope we are creating a legacy, in addition to bottom-line results. While at times it is difficult, it has proven to me that the value of the person I have become is a result of the hours spent learning and living the precepts of the Catholic faith.

Questions for Reflection: *The word* corporation *comes from the Latin root* corpus, *which means "body." What are some ways a corporation can function as one body? List some core values of faith that can inform and nurture the "common good" of a company? Do you know much about Catholic social teaching— which emphasizes the dignity of work and the rights of workers? Where do you find God in your work as a businessperson? How do you balance the need to pay attention to the "bottom line" and to treat co-workers and employees with dignity?*

Chapter 3

A World to Live In: On Being a Catholic Architect

David H. Armitage

My life as an architect began—as all things began—with the story of Genesis, with God's creation of the world, with the coming of light into the darkness. Since childhood, I have found the image of God as architect of the universe immensely compelling. Medieval images of God the architect and, more recently, William Blake's powerful depiction of God the architect remain for me *critical* images of who God is. Few images show God so *at work*, so *human*, as these images. The images depict God thinking, physically active, striding, measuring, contemplating. The writer of Genesis tells us that after each day's work God paused and saw "that it was good," and that on the seventh day, God rested from his labors. We have before us in Genesis the first example of the contemplative person in action and of the active person contemplating. This dynamic, this oscillation back and forth between activity and contemplation, touches on my own experience as an architect.

The story of creation in Genesis can be seen to follow the sequence and pattern of the development of a building. God created something overhead, something underfoot, and then richly decorated it. Even the terminology the writer of Genesis uses reminds us of the components of a building. On the second day of creation, for example, God created the dome of the sky. On the third day, God created dry land, a surface to walk on. After the creation of these larger components, God sat down to the details, to adorning the world with plants and animals of all kinds. Finally, God formed human beings and placed them in his new creation. Out of the void, God created a home, a garden, a safe place for human beings.

Embedded in the story of the creation of the world is the story of the creation of every building. From a formless mass emerges something habitable, beautifully decorated, and safe. The story of creation and of the construction of the world informs my own understanding of the purpose of all buildings: as a shelter from whatever threatens, as a dwelling place, as a home. The Genesis story introduces the important role of "place-making" in God's salvific plan. From Genesis and the creation of the world, to the declaration that "the ground upon which you are walking is holy ground," to the construction of the temple, to the stable, to the tomb, God's participation in the world has often been localized in some *place*. Architects and builders replicate the first instance of building every time they construct.

There is another—*inseparable and preceding*—aspect to the physical creation of the world. Before God's "Let there be light," the writer of Genesis tells us, "a wind from God swept over the face of the waters." For me, this description, this wind, evokes the image of the sheltering wingspread of the hovering Holy Spirit. This was not a one-time event, but preceded creation and continuously protects it. The Jesuit poet Gerard Manley Hopkins reminds us, "Because the Holy Ghost over the bent world broods with warm breast and with ah! bright wings."

These two aspects of the opening paragraphs of Genesis—the physical creation of the world and the spiritual sense of protection and shelter—inform my work as an architect and developer of housing, as well as my personal behavior in the simple events and smallest exchanges of everyday life. At times, I am called on to participate in the creation of physical dwelling places. Other times, however, I am called on to participate in the creation of spiritual places of shelter. The latter is a critical component of the former. In Genesis, spiritual shelter precedes and informs actual physical shelter. I have found that my personal, conceptual experiences of shelter inform the work I do creating actual, physical buildings.

Much of what I know about shelter and housing I learned during the seven years I spent as a Jesuit seminarian. In addition to my studies, my Jesuit training required that I work in a social service setting. I was fortunate to have two important experiences that deeply influence my work as an architect. The first experience came during the period I worked with prostitutes on the west side of Chicago, Illinois, and in Gary, Indiana. The second experience occurred when I worked with children in West Kingston, Jamaica. The first experience didn't involve any building material. The second involved minimal building material. Both experiences, however, touched on fundamental issues of shelter, safety, and belonging. And both were firmly rooted in my life as a person of faith.

As a Jesuit studying philosophy in Chicago, I found myself serving as a counselor to women working as night workers, as prostitutes, in Chicago and Gary. I followed in the footsteps of a Franciscan friar. I learned from this Franciscan that many women who work as night workers do so because they have been literally enslaved by pimps who turn them into utterly dependent drug addicts. To leave a life of prostitution would require a Herculean effort. Recognizing the difficulty for women freely to choose to leave prostitution, and rather than waiting for the unlikely possibility that they would come to him, this Franciscan had learned—and taught me—that it was necessary to *go to* these women wherever they worked. And so I found myself working in the strip joints and adult-only clubs on the west side of Chicago and in Gary.

A customer was required to buy a soda, upon entering one of these places, as a "ticket." As long as I had this ticket, I could stay. Upon receiving my soda, one of the women would approach me and ask me if I wanted some company. This meant I had to give her five dollars for a few minutes of "conversation." The conversation was invariably mild encouragement by the woman to join her in the back room, which meant sixty dollars for half an hour or seventy-five dollars for forty-five minutes. The art of the moment was to spend as much time in conversation and to encourage the women to talk about themselves.

I would always begin by asking each woman if she had any children. Almost all had children and seemed to appreciate the opportunity to talk about them. After several weeks of this same ritual, I was treated as the-guy-who-just-likes-to-talk. Eventually the women didn't even bother to ask me for the five dollars for conversation; they just talked as I listened. I cherish those conversations. I would wait—sometimes for weeks—for the women to say something such as, "I wish I could get out of this business." I would volunteer to look around for them, and arrive the next week with information about a house in Chicago for women who want to leave prostitution. It didn't always happen, but the opportunity was at least there.

The clubs were very dark and, for me, evoked the sense of the world before there was light: vague, formless, a void. It was very hard to see anything. The music was typically loud, pounding, with a sexually suggestive rhythm. The men were from every kind of background, their only bond being a leery, self-conscious, nervous anticipation. In the midst of this primeval, chaotic world, I would listen to the women, leaning in close so as to create a personal, private space between our faces. Together, we would "build" a safe place simply by our attitude of listening and speaking. Without any stone or wood or glass or steel, we created a personal, safe place out of the chaos of the clubs. We were participating in some small way in the creation of order out of chaos. God was with us. For me, it was architecture in its most primitive manifestation. Together, the women and I created a little safe place. I could sense the warm embrace, the bright wings of God's Holy Spirit, hovering around us, protecting us—the essence of shelter.

I remember one woman in particular. Her name was Midnight, and she had three children in foster care. After weeks of quiet, face-to-face conversations, Midnight announced that she was personally going to go before a court the following week to try to get her children out of foster care. She had no lawyer. I volunteered to go with her. I felt it was important to let her know who I was so I asked her, "Midnight, do you know what a Jesuit is?"

"Some kind of priest?" she answered and asked at the same time.

"Yes," I told her.

"Is that what you are?" she asked.

"Yes."

At that moment her name was called; it was her turn to dance. I thought perhaps I shouldn't be there after letting her know who I was and so I began to leave. She touched my arm, "Where are you going?"

"I thought maybe you wouldn't want me here for this."

"No. No, don't go. Please stay. Having you here makes me feel like I have a guardian angel."

§ § §

In Chicago and Gary, I learned about the fundamental nature of space, that is, to provide shelter, a safe place, a haven, from all that threatens. It was pre-material architecture; it was simply the essence of architecture. If my experience in Chicago was pre-material architecture, my experience in Jamaica was barely post-material. In Jamaica, I experienced a housing type that, though simple and light in and of itself, was enormously powerful in its essence.

Most housing in Jamaica is centered around what is commonly known as a Yard. The Jamaican Yard is quite different from the conventional American yard. The Jamaican Yard is the descendent of the house type for slaves in the plantation economy and culture of Jamaica. The 1744 Act of Jamaica required that each slave shanty—a small, one-room hut of unfinished wood and palm fronds—have only one door. Further, each door had to face the home of the plantation owner—called the Great House. The design and configuration of the shanty with its single door was intended to facilitate observation of the movement of slaves by the plantation owner. As a plantation grew, so did the number of shanties. In order to minimize the need for constant vigilance of so many openings, seven-foot walls were built around clusters of six to eight shanties. Again, a single door facing the Great House was built into the seven-foot wall. The intention of the design was to control the slave community. In fact, the opposite happened. The enclosed space provided visual and physical shelter from the plantation owner and enabled the slave population to create, maintain, and pass on their own culture and beliefs. The Yard became the place inside the chaos of the plantation world that provided safety, security, a sense of belonging and of community. To this day, the Yard continues to provide a haven.

While living in West Kingston, I saw countless examples of the social benefit of shanty Yards. West Kingston is a complex web of hundreds of Yards. The streets of West Kingston are essentially canyons, the sides of which are seven-foot-high walls punctuated by doors. Behind the doors are Yards with eight to ten shanty homes. Each home is approximately ten by ten feet. The lineage of the housing type is clear; descriptions of seventeenth-century housing could easily be mistaken for contemporary housing. If the original intent of the housing was to suppress and control, however, Jamaicans have succeeded in transforming the Yard into a mechanism of empowerment and liberation. According to Erna Brodber, a Jamaican sociologist and economist, the shanty/yard phenomenon may very well serve as a therapeutic tool for the internal problems of Jamaica. Yards are the chrysalis out of which rural Jamaicans adapt and move into the city. Yards are the storehouses of laborers that keep the economy moving. Yards provide childcare service for working mothers and operate as basic schools. Yards provide the therapeutic effects of simply chatting and socializing, and are sources of entertainment.

Having grown up in a country of four-bedroom houses with living rooms and dens and playrooms and basement recreation rooms and attics, I was curious to know if Jamaican children found space in their Yards for privacy and personal time. I interviewed a number of schoolchildren and asked them if they found the time and space to wonder and imagine and think about things. *Before* I finished the question, *every* child answered, "Yes." For Duane, a comfortable branch in the breadfruit tree served as his retreat. For Lisa, in the Jamaican *patois* that I love, a "likkle bed" made up in the back seat of an old car gave her time out in her Yard. For Omar, it was a chair behind the shower building where he could "lean bahk and t'ink about t'ings." My exposure to the shanty/yard phenomenon taught me that simple construction is never, in fact, simple. All building is deeply significant and must be handled and considered accordingly.

ᔕ ᔕ ᔕ

These two experiences—both of which emerged out of work associated with my faith life—inform my work as an architect and as a developer of affordable housing. They triggered in me a sense of responsibility to serve people in need of decent shelter. One situation—communicating face to face with another human being—required absolutely no building material, but was critical to understanding the fundamental nature of shelter. The other situation—exposure to a minimalist building type—was packed with meaning and significance.

Both situations were fraught with the essence of shelter, and deeply influence my professional work.

I work as the Director of Design and Construction at the Planning Office for Urban Affairs, the housing development office of the Archdiocese of Boston. I have been working at the Planning Office for four and a half years. Monsignor Michael F. Groden founded the Planning Office in 1969 at the suggestion of then Cardinal Richard Cushing. In thirty years the Planning Office has created over two thousand units of housing at a development cost of over $200 million. Although a substantial number in itself, the emphasis in the office has not been on the number of units created, but rather on precedent-setting forms of housing development. The Planning Office collaborates closely with local, city, state, and federal agencies, and has, over the years, created affordable, quality housing for families and individuals, elderly people, people living with HIV/AIDS, mentally handicapped people, physically disabled people. Our developments are open to people regardless of race, nationality, gender, sexual orientation, and religion.

The Planning Office is relatively small, considering the number of projects it sponsors. Although each person in our seven-person office has an individual profession, we all share in the varied tasks development work demands. I sometimes liken what each of us does to the role of a symphony orchestra conductor. One section of the orchestra, for example, is the community process, another section is the architectural design, another the construction, another the city permitting process, and yet another section of the orchestra is the financing of the project. The art of our work is to keep each piece moving in the right direction, at the appropriate pace according to the specific phase of development. For example, early on it is important to focus on the community process, and to keep the contractor ready in the background. Later in the development process, it is important to bring in the contractor, and to move on from the community process. Development work is a complex, sophisticated process of coordination and communication. It is easy to become disillusioned by the process and thereby lose sight of the purpose of our work: to provide safe, attractive, affordable housing.

The current economy and demographic patterns mean that it is next to impossible for a family or individual of moderate means to live in Boston. The labor infrastructure, the very people who enable the city to run—teachers, firemen and women, policemen and women, hospital workers, city workers, hotel workers, transportation workers—cannot afford to live in the city. Working closely with city and state agencies to address the problem, the Planning Office is currently creating a development that is 60 percent affordable. In a field where 10 percent affordable is the norm, it is a remarkable achievement. It is a source of enormous satisfaction to be working for the archdiocese and for men like Monsignor Groden, who has an extraordinary ability to push projects forward despite colossal odds, and for Cardinal Bernard Law, whose daring leadership in this area is unparalleled.

The Our Father tells us "Thy kingdom come, thy will be done, *on earth*, as it is in heaven." All human beings, as children of God, are called to participate in God's ongoing creation of order out of disorder. We are called to create a world of love and compassion out of a world that is often chaotic and threatening. In a world full of distractions, it is easy to lose sight of this. But, I have found, the experiences that have emerged out of my faith life help me to stay focused, to stay the course, and to maintain sight of the mission. The face-to-face contact with women like Midnight brings homelessness and loneliness and fear right into my world. I take these experiences, hold them before me always, and allow them to inform my work. My faith and my work are inextricably entwined. When I become tired or disillusioned, I remember Midnight. Then all seems luminous to me.

Questions for Reflection: *In what ways is God the "first architect"? How would you define "physical space" and "spiritual space"—how are they similar? How are they different? What are some of the physical places and spaces that help you connect with the sacred? How does your faith help you to see the sacred in the spaces of the world—from physical buildings like cathedrals to spiritual connections like friendship? How can we serve as "architects" who co-create sacred spaces with God?*

Chapter 4

Justice from a Higher Power: On Being a Catholic Police Officer

John A. Eterno

The chapter that follows was written before the terrorist attacks of September 11, 2001, which destroyed the World Trade Center towers in New York City, severely damaged the Pentagon in Washington, D.C., and took the lives of brave passengers who, in fighting the terrorists who had seized their plane, crashed in a field in Pennsylvania. I wish to express my deepest sympathies to the families, friends, and acquaintances of those who were killed. Other than the addition of this introduction, however, I have not changed a single word of this piece. I believed then as I do now that God is with us in everything, and that, no matter how difficult, our faith in God is what helps us sustain the kind of hope and compassion that helps us to be our very best.

For those of us in New York City, the appalling atrocity of September 11 was only outweighed by the enormous, selfless bravery of police, firefighters, medics, rescue workers, and so many others. The fallout from the attacks is exactly the type of situation that first responders, including police officers, are trained to handle. And I believe that these first responders, and all who helped and were killed, were following in the footsteps of our Lord Jesus. That is, none of them died in vain; their lives give us life. These officers were servants of righteousness, performing their trained duty in the most trying of circumstances, helping and literally saving others.

As you will read in this essay, faith in Jesus Christ guides me in my daily life. At times it can be difficult to act on faith, especially as a police officer, but God always gives us the strength we need to persevere. Let us all hope and pray that the world will be a more tolerant and peaceful place. May God bless America and each and every one of us.

§ § §

Pain, agony, depression, sickness, crime, death—police officers in New York City are unique in that they are constantly exposed to the maladies of life. People do not call police officers to advise them of new births or other happy events; rather, police officers are called to deal with the unwanted, the rejected, the mentally ill, the criminal, those in pain, or those who have died. New York City police officers are charged with the daunting task of properly handling the morbid aspects of life. To accomplish this task, Catholic police officers are armed with much more than special training and a gun—they take with them into the streets, homes, offices, workplaces, and all other areas of the city the lessons given to us by faith.

For all Catholics, and especially police officers, practicing the fundamentals of the Catholic faith can be very difficult in our day-to-day lives. It means holding back anger and frustration, respecting the dignity of all people including those who are hurting others or not respecting others, dealing with death and dying on a regular basis, serving others in any way that we can, and—most of all—loving others.

Loving others sums up how our faith teaches us to deal with people on a day-to-day basis. For example, in Matthew 22:37–40 there is a lesson in a scene where a Pharisee tries to trap Jesus:

> "Teacher, which commandment in the law is the greatest?" He said to him, "'You shall love the Lord your God with all your heart, and with all your soul, and with all your mind.' This is the greatest and first commandment. And a second is like it: 'You shall love your neighbor as yourself.' On these two commandments hang all the law and the prophets."

This one lesson of faith is enough to last a lifetime! God's lesson of love is easy to understand, yet it can be so very difficult to follow. In practice, this means, for example, that regardless of a person's race, class, gender, or other status, we must love that person. Does this mean the criminal? Yes. Does this mean the emotionally disturbed? Yes. Does this mean the rejected? Yes. Does this mean someone who is trying to harm us? Yes!

As Catholic police officers, we are called to treat every person, even those who are breaking the law, with the dignity and respect that he or she deserves merely for being human. We believe that every person is created and loved by God. We must love every person, even those who are criminals and enemies of society. As a police officer, I find this truly challenging. I recall, for example, working in the Tenth Precinct on the west side of Manhattan in New York City's Chelsea area. It was a warm night and the city streets were crowded with people. Around midnight, my partner and I were on our way to the precinct in a marked radio car. On the way, I noticed a crowd gathered outside a local bar. Looking closer, I observed a man with a gun in the middle of the crowd. I recalled that the precinct had received many calls about a man with a gun at that same bar, but because the calls were so numerous and none of the officers deployed to the scene had ever found the man with the gun, we thought we were getting bad information or that someone was lying. This situation, however, was obviously real. Apparently, this gunman was consistently eluding police. I told my partner, who initially thought I was joking, that a man with a gun was standing outside the bar. Once he realized the situation was quite serious, he immediately stopped the radio car. We both quickly exited the car, our minds completely focused on the job at hand.

Since my partner was driving, I was closer to the suspect and in a better position to take action. I unholstered my revolver and pointed it directly at the suspect shouting, "Police! Don't move!" I was seriously concerned about the safety of the crowd of patrons standing around him. The suspect then pointed his gun in my direction! However, he did not seem to be aiming or wanting to shoot. I held back and somehow neither I nor my partner fired our weapons. I continued to approach the suspect while advising him not to move. He began to raise his hands. When I was about three or four steps away, in one quick movement, I lurched toward the armed man and grabbed the gun from his hands. Then, I placed him against a nearby wall to frisk him for other weapons. It all happened so quickly, in less than a minute. Afterwards we discovered that the man was involved in a bar fight and was using the gun to threaten his opponent. I believe what made the difference between shooting and not shooting the armed man was respect for human life, both the suspect's and the crowd's. This respect is ingrained into a practicing Catholic's life; indeed, it is a cornerstone of the Catholic faith. And this respect generally remains with a Catholic even in tense moments as I have described.

Treating every person with dignity and respect, regardless of their background, can be very difficult. However, most situations in which we are challenged to act as our faith dictates are not as dramatic as the previously described incident. Nevertheless, these can be just as difficult and perhaps, in the long term, even more important. We are particularly challenged in everyday situations where faith teaches us differently from the common culture. Before his death, Cardinal John O'Connor used the words of Pope John Paul II to describe contemporary culture as a "culture of death." In the United States, for example, abortion is accepted as normal, as evidenced by our laws. As Catholics, we are called to reject this cultural norm. We strive to change the norm such that human life is respected in all its forms. This does not mean that we violate the law, but rather that we respect the law and work within it to change what we disagree with. If you are honest with yourself, you will realize that this type of change is exceedingly difficult to accomplish. In your life, for example, recall a time when your friends and/or family were discussing something controversial. Perhaps they were speaking of abortion or birth control and how they think these things are necessary today. Did you enter the conversation and say "that's wrong" and explain why? Whether you did or not is not really the issue. The point is that living a life of love and faith can truly be a challenge, and we are called to live out our faith as authentically as possible.

As Catholics, and in my case as a Catholic police officer, we are called to live out our faith *all the time*—not just when it is convenient, but even when it goes against the culture and/or common practice. By virtue of the job, police officers often must do the opposite of others. For example, most people run from a person with a gun; police officers go toward the person. Many people avoid large, rowdy gatherings; police are charged with keeping them orderly. In sum, police officers put their lives on the line to protect and serve others—going against common practice and a culture that basically states, "save yourself at all cost, even at the cost of others' lives."

Some aspects of the culture are detrimental to police officers. The common culture often stereotypes police officers as disrespectful of life. For example, police officers are often portrayed as violent thugs willing to use force to counter almost any violation. Nothing could be further from the truth. Officers are rigorously trained to use the minimum amount of force necessary and to use deadly physical force (that is, to shoot) only when one's own life or the life of another is in danger. The fact that police shootings are very rare indeed is a testament to the fine training given at most police academies in which the stereotypical image of the cop is replaced with a more realistic image—a professional, service-oriented police officer. Unfortunately, however, if a person enters an academy without a basic rudimentary understanding and belief of the importance of life, the lessons may never take hold.

For Catholics, these qualities—especially respect for life—are constantly reinforced. Those who frequently attend Mass, in particular, are constantly strengthened and reminded of the importance of every human being. This occurs not only during the homily (where the priest expounds on previously read Scripture readings, often pointing out its practical meaning and importance), but throughout the Mass. Thus, the celebration of the Eucharist—which prepares us to receive the body and blood of our Lord—obliges us to reflect on our own lives (in order to be properly prepared to receive), reinforcing respect for human life and other aspects of our faith.

Police officers must not only contend with the pressures of the culture in general but also face many other pressures from the work environment. This includes contending with what is called the "police culture." The police culture is sometimes referred to as the informal code to distinguish it from formal rules. The police culture emphasizes the importance of the group, the influence of peers—that is, other officers. Indeed, common euphemisms such as the "blue wall of silence" or "testilying" certainly suggest that the police culture is able to defy organization guidelines, community norms, and legal constraints, and even promotes wrongful behavior. Catholic police officers, as disciples of love, try to overcome these negative influences and stand up for what is right.

In essence, this means setting an example; we must transform beliefs (our faith) into actions (and actions speak much louder than words). We cannot blindly follow our peers, especially when our peers are violating basic Catholic teaching. I recall an incident, when I was working in the Midtown North Precinct, that serves as an excellent illustration of how difficult it can be to practice the Catholic faith as a police officer. The incident occurred in the late evening in the precinct holding-pen area (where prisoners are held during arrest processing). At the time, a young rookie police officer had just arrested four male prostitutes who were being processed for violating the law. One of the more experienced police officers in the precinct was upsetting the prisoners by taunting them (for what reason, I do not know). The experienced officer was shouting obscenities and threatening prisoners, and soon began to physically approach them. The rookie was unable to deal with the situation as the prisoners began to get more and more upset. It was apparent that the older officer would soon be engaged in fisticuffs with these prisoners.

The rookie obviously needed help. It was merely happenstance that I was passing near the holding-pen area. I peered inside and immediately realized the need to interject both in the rookie's defense and to maintain the peace. After separating the experienced officer from the prisoners, I advised the experienced officer that it would be better to leave the prisoners to the arresting officer. He was somewhat belligerent but seemed to back off from me—probably because I was simply not as intimidated as the rookie was. Let me remind you, however, that at the time I was the same rank as the experienced officer. Although the experienced officer left, without any harm done, the situation could have been tragic. I remained with the rookie officer until he calmed down and realized everything was fine. He continually thanked me the entire time I was with him.

This was a very difficult situation for me (and, I supposed, for the rookie officer). I could have chosen not to get involved, to let the experienced officer abuse the prisoners. However, I did what I thought was right. Most importantly, as Catholics, we must learn that all people, regardless of their background or what they have done, deserve respect. These

John A. Eterno

were prisoners, male prostitutes, who needed protection from a misguided officer. It was not easy for me to intercede; it went against a basic cultural norm (i.e., "mind your own business"). Nevertheless, it was the right thing to do.

This is often the dilemma that we have as Catholics. Our faith requires us to take action but that action may be difficult and go against common culture and practice. Nevertheless, this is our calling—to live a life of love. Regardless of the level of difficulty, we believe that God will give us the strength to act appropriately.

As police offices and Catholics we cannot stand idly by while others are in pain or are working to alleviate that pain. We see this in Matthew 23: 4–6, 11–12:

> They tie up heavy burdens, hard to bear, and lay them on the shoulders of others; but they themselves are unwilling to lift a finger to move them. They do all their deeds to be seen by others . . . They love to have the place of honor at banquets and the best seats in the synagogues . . . [Rather] the greatest among you will be your servent. All who exalt themselves will be humbled, and all who humble themselves will be exalted.

To Catholic police officers—of all ranks—this means, quite literally, that we are servants. We serve the public, our

51

subordinates on the job, our families, our communities, our bosses—and most importantly our Lord, Jesus Christ. We should be shining examples of what it means to serve. This means not lording whatever power we have been given over others but rather to bring God's peace to all around us.

What an example Jesus is for us! Recall how he washes his disciples' feet at the Last Supper. He, the Lord and Creator of all, washing feet! It is absolutely astonishing. Also, recall his dying and acceptance of death in a most demeaning way, on a cross! This is complete obedience to the Father! This is what is asked of all Catholics—perhaps, not as dramatically, nevertheless similarly.

In particular, Catholic police officers are called to a life of love, service, and obedience. Although very few police officers are called upon to give their lives in the performance of their duty, those who do—and as difficult as that is—are following the footsteps of our Lord. This is the epitome of what it means to love, serve, and obey. As John 15:13 quotes Jesus, "No one has greater love than this, to lay down one's life for one's friends."

Most police officers, fortunately, do not have to make this ultimate sacrifice. As Catholics, however, we must still strive to emulate our Savior. This often means sacrifice, but of a different nature. Like many other Catholics today, we may have to change some career goals to improve our relationships with our families and others. I see many colleagues taking care of children or trying to help with elderly parents who may be ill. This, combined with the pressures of the job, can be very demanding. Something, somewhere must give. Often, this leads to a change of assignment—from a highly visible crime-fighting position to something less time consuming. This can be very damaging to one's career.

Conversely, the family—unfortunately—often sacrifices for the occupation as well. Being married to a New York City police officer carries with it many burdens. For example, in New York City, police officers' salaries are not as lucrative as one might expect. This means doing with less or officers working second, third, or more jobs while off duty (taking away from quality time with family). This also adds to the pressures at home and at work. It is likely that such stress adds to the very high rate of divorce and suicide among New York City police.

In sum, as Catholic police officers we try to set an example of servitude. We must balance home, work, and other responsibilities. Most importantly, our priorities are to love God and to love others. This is a challenging task, especially for police officers who often work with people who are rejected by society. The culture of our society and the culture of police can hinder our faith, but we try to overcome these obstacles. This can be done most effectively by practicing our faith—especially receiving the Eucharist regularly. This reinforces and strengthens us.

Among all these responsibilities, the most important is to find time for God. It is Jesus who blesses our homes, our labor, our lifestyle such that it is productive. It is he who guides and protects us. It is he in whom our trust lies. To Catholic police officers of faith, there is no choice but to follow Jesus, even when it is not palatable. As Peter states in John 6:68, "Lord, to whom can we go? You have the words of eternal life."

Questions for Reflection: *Police officers are called upon to protect and serve. Given the challenges and dangers of police work, how can faith inform an officer's work? What does it mean to love others, including your enemies? What does Pope John Paul II mean when he refers to the modern era as a "culture of death"? How can Catholics help transform this culture into one of life? How is the Mass a part of your life as a Catholic? On a daily basis, what are some of the issues that confront Catholics trying to live according to their faith?*

Chapter 5

One Case at a Time: On Being a Catholic Lawyer

Amelia J. Uelmen

I work as a lawyer in a large law firm that serves, for the most part, large corporations. When enumerating professions that would seem to leave the most room to integrate one's faith, this occupation, and particularly this context, is not at the top of anyone's list. In fact, many would write it off as completely hopeless.

Here's the image: lawyers are hopelessly entangled in greed—just click onto internet chat-rooms where twenty-six-year-old "greedyassociates" whine about the inadequacy of their six-figure salaries. Hopelessly numbed by long grueling hours of dull and meaningless work under the pressure of stressful deadlines—billing the time to support those six-figure salaries. Hopelessly entrenched in the interests of big business, which, for the most part, has divorced itself from a sense of responsibility to the local and global community.

I am not going to say that there is no truth to this image.

But I am going to start by asking the reader a favor: set this image aside, at least for the next few minutes—and imagine with me that there is hope for integrating the demanding challenges of faith even into this profession, even into this kind of legal practice.

What do attorneys at large law firms do all day? Generally, they specialize in an area of legal service to large businesses. They focus on the characteristics of their agreements, negotiations, development, and growth; on their interactions with government regulatory agencies and with the public; or, in litigation, on what may have gone wrong in these various relationships.

If we move beyond the image of lawyer as "hired gun," I believe many aspects of this kind of practice can be characterized, in and of themselves, as neutral. To qualify the effects of a lawyer's work, we must examine each case in context—each aspect of a lawyer's work can be used to keep the status quo humming along, used as a tool for social destruction, or used as a channel for dialogue about social responsibility.

What kinds of people, what kinds of lawyers, could and do use legal service to large businesses as the opener for a dialogue about social responsibility? I am going to focus on two kinds that are helpful in this effort. First, people who are ready to ask serious questions about the social structures while working right in the thick of them; and who have the courage to speak about and, where possible, apply alternative values that may run contrary to those structures. Second, and linked to the first, people who are able to create and maintain as a priority a vital connection to communities that foster alternative values and through which to maintain a sense of service—through skills as a lawyer and involvement as a person.

Developing and keeping this kind of perspective in the context of legal practice at a large firm is challenging. What follows is a little bit about my own daily efforts, which I hope you find useful in thinking creatively about applying these principles to your own life and work.

I have found much in my Catholic tradition to guide my efforts to integrate faith into my professional life. I keep taped to my computer this piece from *Gaudium et Spes*, the Second Vatican Council's "Pastoral Constitution on the Church in the Modern World":

> By nature the human person stands completely in need of life in society; the human person ought to be the beginning, the subject, and the end of every social

organization. Life in society is not something acces-
sory to the human person; through our dealings with
others, through mutual service, and through dialogue, we develop all our talents and become able to
rise to our destiny (no. 25).

In the context of legal practice at a large firm, what
does it mean to keep the human person at the center of every
social organization, and to see life in society—in particular,
my work life—as a channel for fulfillment as a human being?

I have found helpful insight on this through involvement in the Focolare Movement, an international Catholic
organization that is working for unity and dialogue between
people of different cultures, races, social backgrounds, and religious traditions. Its spirituality encourages people to integrate
gospel values into all aspects of everyday life, in the family, in
school, in the workplace. I thought, why not in a big business
context, too? So I began practice in a large law firm hoping not
only to gain something—a nuanced understanding of the
complexities of civil litigation and of what makes the business
world tick—but also to contribute something—the effort to
weave a set of spiritual values into my daily work.

I spent the first six months somewhat afraid—of what
people were thinking, of what they expected, of whether I
could trudge up the steep learning curve . . . and becoming

very, very tired. Everything around me seemed to scream that the key to success is to be, think, and act as others expect. Then, talking through these concerns with some close friends, two treasures came into light, which have since anchored my approach to practice.

First, learn to listen to and be guided by the voice of God within—take the time and make the effort to distinguish it from external pressures and circumstances—and then follow what it suggests. Second, make every effort, and at any cost, to hang onto some semblance of a balanced life that enables one to nourish the values that guide one's life.

To be guided by the voice of God within, for me went hand in hand with an effort to live, to apply to everyday situations in the office, the words of Scripture. Just a few examples, as applied to relationships with colleagues.

I'll never forget the day I realized how the phrase "Perfect love casts out fear" (1 Jn. 4:18) could transform the relationship with the partner supervising my work. In the context of research for appellate briefs, I discovered that "perfect love" meant not only thoroughness and creativity but also sincerity and honesty in presenting my legal analysis, even if it wasn't the answer my supervisor was hoping for. Over time, I understood how this approach helped me to bring a fully responsible contribution to projects, even as a very junior lawyer.

Applying "Love your neighbor as yourself" (Leviticus 19:18, Matthew 22:39) led and continues to lead to the precious capacity to let go of my own ego, of the competitive drive to chalk up credit and approval—and instead, to look for and create opportunities to weave in values of cooperation, to foster relationships of encouragement and respect, in order to build a sense of community.

In the ups and downs of office politics, "Blessed are the merciful, for they will receive mercy" (Matthew 5:7) has been an important key to resolving conflicts and disagreements. In situations where I felt people had hurt me, I could give them another chance, try to see the situation from their perspective so we could heal and rebuild the relationships to the point that we could work well together.

And the "mercy" returns: under the stress and pressure of filing deadlines, in moments when my irritability or impatience had hurt others, the reminder to "leave your gift there before the altar and go; first be reconciled to your brother" (Matthew 5:24) is a push to apologize before the day's end, often opening up better channels of communication and leading to more profound friendships.

As for troubling questions about the big economic structures from which big firm associates draw their paychecks? "Just as you did it to one of the least of these . . . you do it to me" (Matthew 25:40) is for me a constant reminder of the presence of God in each person—including each person affected by how large corporations do business. Have I as a junior, and now as a mid-level litigator, been in a position to influence the decisions of corporate executives in this regard? No. In fact, in my work on large, complex products-liability cases, I have never even met the in-house counsel liaison.

What can associates with little voice and little power do? Let me offer just a few ideas. First, we can encourage the seeds of social responsibility which are already germinating—for example, many big firms pour thousands of dollars in resources and financial and business expertise into *pro bono* projects that assist community organizations and the poor with their legal needs. Skyrocketing salaries are a direct threat to this commitment—time set aside for *pro bono* work may be pushed aside by the pressure to bill more hours in order to support the higher salaries. Now is the time for associates to be especially vocal about their concerns, to be ready to make less money rather than sacrifice this commitment to the community, and to vote with their feet when firms renege on this commitment.

Second, in many firms it is possible to find lawyers in positions of influence who do premise their advice and advocacy on a strong sense of responsibility to the larger community. We can appreciate and encourage their efforts, and learn from them.

Third, we can generate challenging internal conversations. In fact, one may be surprised by the level of openness and profound moral reflection found among people with complex and varied reasons for spending some time in big firm practice. In addition, many junior attorneys with little voice and power today eventually assume positions of influence and responsibility—as partners, in large corporations' legal departments, in the government, in non-legal business jobs. Even if it seems that not much headway is being made, keeping the wheels turning with ideas for how alternative values can challenge large businesses to a deeper sense of social responsibility may be important for the future.

What are the costs? Almost certainly, being teased for marching to the beat of a different drummer. Probably being somewhat misunderstood. In super-conformist environments, the chance of being completely ostracized. But it is worth it, I think, in light of the consequent ability to live a consistent and integrated life. In fact, I have seen how these kinds of choices often generate a certain respect and create a solid basis for sincere collegial relationships.

And now the $64,000 question—or given the salaries, the $164,000 question—in large firms where the working conditions for many lawyers are anything but conducive to keeping touch with alternative values: If you are working between sixty and eighty hours a week, and for many, simultaneously juggling family responsibilities, how can you find the time or energy for social responsibility?

I have found that by far the biggest challenge in legal practice at a large firm is not the lack of openness to conversations about social responsibility. It is insisting on the necessity of maintaining the balanced life that enables one to hang on to this kind of perspective. It is claiming the time to keep the relationships with family and friends healthy and alive; the time to pray, to take a lunch break, to put some order in the house, to keep horizons of study beyond the narrow borders of one's legal specialization; and absolutely crucial, the time for a meaningful connection to one's faith community.

Very early on, I realized that if I were to become unplugged from this sense of balance, I would have no energy, no light, and no guts to be a person who loves, who lives the gospel in a law firm environment. So I formed and began to work with a set of internal definitions: for example, dinner at home is normal; dinner at work should be extraordinary. And, to use legal jargon, a "rebuttable presumption" that weekends are mine—my time to maintain this balance and connection to the community.

I dug in my heels. Explain to me, what is the court deadline that makes you insist this project is due tonight instead of tomorrow (i.e., keeping me from dinner at home) or Monday morning instead of Wednesday (i.e., ruining my weekend). And if it is because this is what it takes to serve this client well, then I have another question: Have we really made every effort to adequately staff this case, and to cooperate and share information, so that this can be done in the most efficient way? If we have taken all of these steps, fine—I'll stay, and rework my plans. If not, why not?

Depending on the circumstances, sometimes I stayed. Most of the time I did not. For all the times I did not stay, I believe that I was a better, more capable, and more efficient lawyer when I came into work fresh on Monday morning. But where firm profits are contingent on "billable" hours—and in some firms, on squeezing as many billable hours out of associates as possible—this is hardly the shortcut to partnership. It might be difficult for firms to figure out what to do with a perceived lack of commitment and interest in taking the kind of responsibility needed to assume leadership within the firm, all considered as handicaps to one's full development as a lawyer.

It is probably worth noting that at least in this kind of economy, I did not get fired. I was able to work out an arrangement of less money for fewer hours. In fact, a few firms have recently instituted salary structures in which associates may choose to work fewer hours for less money.

Here, too, skyrocketing salaries are a direct threat to any hope for a balanced life. We need a critical mass of associates to stand up and say, "Keep your money; you don't own every waking hour of my life." But as the fallout from the recent "salary wars" indicates, this critical mass does not yet exist. Why not? Greed? Perhaps partially—especially in the stage following payment of astronomical student debt. After a few years of earning a six-figure salary, some may find it difficult to unlock themselves from the "golden handcuffs" of comfortable wealth.

But I believe that a scratch beneath the surface reveals a deeper problem—lack of hope, lack of conviction that the structures can really change. So more money becomes a kind of consolation prize: If I must work these kind of hours, at least I'm getting paid at the same rate as my classmates working at the firm down the street.

What might bring an injection of hope, of conviction that the stakes are too high to settle for consolation prizes? It helps to be connected to people who are capable of imagining something different, working towards that transformation, and ready to pay the costs. As for the day-to-day life in the trenches, perhaps one of the greatest signs of hope is simply to be a person who tries with creativity, courage, and determination to "give it all" rather than "have it all"—and who shines with the joy, the freedom, and the fulfillment that come from the effort.

Questions for Reflection: *Many professions have earned a reputation for serving the bottom line at all costs; an employee's time is valuable only when it translates into more money for the company. In what ways does faith challenge the notions that "time is money" and the bottom line is the only goal for a business? What do Scripture and the Catholic tradition teach us about talents, time, and community? How can faith inspire and sustain one's efforts to challenge, and even change, social structures? Why is it important to find a faith community? How might you find time for "social responsibility"? The Second Vatican Council document* Gaudium et Spes *is one example of how church teaching helps guide daily life. What other encyclicals, documents, and teachings have you found helpful in daily life?*

Chapter 6

The Good News: On Being a Catholic Journalist

Terry Golway

A few years ago, on a Monday morning just before Election Day, a newsroom colleague asked me if I had watched a particular Sunday morning political talk show the day before. Somebody had said something that seemed amazingly newsworthy at the time, but now, of course, I can no longer remember the speaker, the name of his or her interrogator, the statement itself, or the precise year in which the statement was made.

I replied that I hadn't. "Why not?" my colleague asked with a mixture of frustration and downright contempt. No doubt he was entertaining the idea that I had slept in on

Sunday morning and thus was derelict in my journalistic duties.

"I was in church," I told him. Contempt and frustration gave way to something resembling the look that probably crossed Margaret Mead's face when she came upon various exotic inhabitants of the South Pacific.

"You go to church?" he asked. "I don't know anybody who still goes to church."

I later learned that my colleague's sister is a nun, which suggests that the two of them need to communicate a little better.

Nevertheless, my colleague's astonishment at finding a churchgoer in his midst was not out of place. Although the name of Jesus Christ is frequently invoked in America's newsrooms, particularly as deadline approaches, journalists are not the most religious or spiritual of souls. Skepticism, irreverence and iconoclasm are the hammer and tongs of the journalism trade, and, as many journalists consider themselves on the job 24/7, they are rarely without the tools of their profession. They tend to view religious dogma as just another campaign platform, and religious leaders as politicians. Journalists get paid to ask tough questions, and they presume (not without reason) that the answers they get are lies or half-truths. Faith is not part of the professional vocabulary.

Of course, journalism isn't the only profession so imbued with skepticism. Scholars and academics also are required to probe, to question, to doubt. But it's hard to imagine, perhaps because I know so many Ph.D.s who are deeply religious, that academics are as avowedly non-religious as any random collection of ten newspaper, broadcast, or magazine journalists. Then again, I haven't spent a whole lot of time on campus in recent years.

I have, however, spent every year since 1973 in a newsroom, and, consequently, I've met hundreds of journalists from all races, creeds, and backgrounds. I doubt that more than a dozen would consider themselves religious (as opposed to being spiritual, a category that would include perhaps a few dozen more). And, for a few years when I was getting started in the journalism business, I wouldn't have considered myself particularly religious, either. At the same time, I wasn't completely immersed in the professional culture of skepticism and doubt, and certainly knew people—including family members—who practiced their faith. In retrospect, that may be why, in the mid-1980s, a reporter-colleague who was a born-again Christian (talk about a minority) invited me to join her church. I declined as gently as I could, and we subsequently had several conversations in which the name of Jesus was invoked in more reverential terms than is customary in a newsroom. It would be hard to imagine a more atypical newsroom experience.

My work as a newspaper reporter for nearly thirty years has never been at cross purposes with my faith, although I suspect that my Catholic-school upbringing may have made me a little more respectful of authority than the average journalist. Once, some years ago, I was talking with a colleague about a politician suspected of involvement in some dubious dealings. I argued that the politician probably was innocent because, after all, he had denied his involvement so forcefully.

"He lied," my colleague said. "They all do."

I remember being shocked—this was a long time ago—by the assumption and the generalization. All these years later, I'm still more surprised than I should be when politicians and other authority figures are caught lying, cheating, or stealing. Perhaps, in middle age, I'm still as naive as a teenager. Or perhaps, because I go to church and am taught to see Christ in every human being, I lack the famous edge journalists are supposed to have. I tend to give the people I write about the benefit of the doubt, a trait that is not, shall we say, shared by most journalists.

As a person of faith, I believe my work can't help but reflect the values we associate with religious belief in general and certainly Catholic teaching in particular—hope, charity (well, at least on occasion!), a passion for social justice, a sense of equity in temporal affairs. My faith has led me to write columns questioning the dogma of globalism and unfettered markets and to assail Princeton University's hiring of Peter Singer, who thinks we shouldn't kill animals but can kill babies with hemophilia, as a professor of bioethics. My columns, I like to think, serve as a witness to religious belief, even though the topics generally are secular. And I hope my behavior in the newsroom, while frequently in keeping with horrid stereotypes (at the moment I'm staring at a half-full bottle of whiskey on my desk), betrays at least an inkling of the values I treasure as part of my Catholicism.

Conservatives often charge that America's newsrooms are filled with liberals who are either openly hostile or secretly suspicious of competing political ideologies. That may or may not be true (it's a mix), but rest assured that it is easier to find a conservative in a newsroom than a regular churchgoer. Rarer still is a born-again Christian, like my former colleague, or an Orthodox Jew.

That said, I don't think that journalists who are religious, who practice their faith, are discriminated against, ostracized, or otherwise made to feel like outcasts. They certainly are the object of some curiosity and perhaps the occasional "can you believe it" whisper. I've worked in newsrooms where people have assumed that because I practice my faith, Catholicism, I can therefore answer questions about all faiths:

"Hey, Golway," the editor barks (editors always bark), "you go to church, so you'll know this. What's the difference between a Methodist and a Lutheran? Would the Lubavitchers be considered Zionists?" That's harmless enough, I suppose.

More insidious, though, is the ignorance that comes from such an agnostic culture. Because journalists themselves work with—and socialize with—very few people who practice a traditional religion, they have little understanding of those who do. Even today, the model for covering churchgoers is H. L. Mencken, whose vivid dismissals of Southern backwoods fundamentalism are part of America's journalistic canon. Today's journalists, for the most part, don't know much more about the lives of religious people than Mencken did, but that doesn't stop them from perpetuating stereotypes.

Consequently, at a time when almost every facet of Americans' lives is now fit for discussion in the media, the astonishing breadth, vitality, and diversity of religious life in America is relatively unexplored. Of the approximate 1,500 daily newspapers in America, only about 250 have a religion beat. Public broadcasting recently developed a program called "Religion and Ethics Newsweekly," but it generally is shown at some, er, ungodly hour. Several years ago, ABC News announced the appointment of a full-time religion reporter, but other networks have not followed suit (an unusual development in television news). Worse yet, when religion is covered in some way, it's usually for all the wrong reasons: a clerical sex scandal; a controversial political pronouncement; a misappropriation of funds; a terrorist act carried out in the name of twisted dogma.

Journalists, because they like being thought of as persnickety and counterintuitive, sometimes delight in viewing religion as a divisive force in society, and regarding its practitioners as intolerant, ignorant, and superstitious. Never mind that sometimes religious people give such critics ample material to justify prejudices. If there were more people of faith in the journalism business, journalists very likely would be more inclined to view religious belief as an integral part of the communities they cover. They would be less likely to make sweeping judgments about churchgoers. And they certainly would never write, as one left-wing commentator did during the impeachment crisis of 1998, that a "Catholic Mafia" in the media was deploying its "absolutist" sensibility to help bring down Bill Clinton. This hate-filled generalization was gross on any number of counts. To cite just two: the use of the term "Catholic Mafia" (as if American Catholicism is a monolith) and the suggestion that all Catholics, because of their "absolutism," believed that Bill Clinton should have been removed from office. Hold on, now: Wasn't Bill Clinton's counsel an Irish-Catholic guy named Jack Quinn?

Sentiments like these, I must say, are not uncommon among the high-end media in New York, and it is New York that sets the tone for media elsewhere. I've heard more than a few derogatory comments about religion in general and Catholicism in particular in my twelve years at the *New York Observer*, a weekly that covers the Manhattan "power elite." And those comments have turned me into something of a Catholic nationalist. I don't write regularly about religion in my columns and feature articles in the avowedly secular *Observer*, but I regard it as part of my mission to point out to the newspaper's elite readers that I am a Catholic, that I go to church, that my kids attend Catholic school. I've written a bit about the positions the American bishops have taken on social justice issues, precisely because so many journalists and their New York audiences prefer to think of American Catholicism as rigid and reactionary. I've written about the astonishing diversity of American and worldwide Catholicism, pointing out that if ever there was an example of multiculturalism at work, it is the Roman Catholic Church.

None of this political combat, of course, has much to do with faith and spirituality. But it does do wonders for the relief of headaches, heartburn, and various other newsroom ailments.

Questions for Reflection: *How comfortable are you talking about faith, religion, and spirituality in your own circles at school and/or work? What are some of the challenges associated with living as a Catholic in the modern world? While an overwhelming majority of Americans claim to believe in God, why is religion such a small part of the daily news coverage? How can people of faith balance jobs like journalism that require objectivity and even skepticism? What are some creative ways that you might apply the convictions of faith to everyday life?*

Chapter 7

Flesh of My Flesh: On Being a Catholic Spouse

Sidney Callahan

"Hell is not to love any more madam. Not to love any more!" So speaks the young curate to the Countess, in Bernanos's great novel *The Diary of a Country Priest*. The Countess hates her daughter (who reciprocates), despises her philandering husband, and has hardened her heart against God since the death of her only beloved son. But all the while, she takes pride in "never having failed a single duty," religious or social.

This cold callousness pushes the holy young priest to the sad reflection, "Of all hate, domestic hate is the most dangerous, it assuages itself by perpetual conflict, it is like those open abscesses without fever which slowly poison . . . families frighten me." And well they should.

Fear is a healthy response for married Christians to have. Who is not afraid of letting love curdle into lethargy and deadening boredom? The all-encompassing intimacy of marriage need not produce domestic hate, but it always uncovers every lapse and failure of love. Marriage puts charity to the ultimate test. There's no place to hide, no cell into which to withdraw, no privacy. Every sin and error directly affects another and is exposed. Not only must the spouse be patient and kind, hopeful and enduring, as in St. Paul's famous passage on benevolent charity in 13 Corinthians, but a good spouse must also cultivate *eros* and be an ardent lover—until death do us part. *Eros* is a love that is a passionate preference for the particular, unique, embodied person. My spouse is bone of my bone, flesh of my flesh—in sickness and health, for better or worse.

For Worse

Marriage can be hell. Sartre famously observed that "hell is other people," but after reading Bernanos, we would have to amend the description to say that hell is other people whom you cannot love. Yet, Christians have an all-purpose remedy. No matter what happens in a marriage, believers can call upon Christ the physician for healing. Seeking contrition for one's own sins makes it possible to forgive the wrongs and wounds inflicted by every spouse in every marriage. The Church lets us know that marriage as a sacrament will be an encounter with Christ, so marital partners can confidently call upon the Holy Spirit to strengthen and support them in any difficulty. And almost every marriage will have times when it needs help. Maybe there are some blissfully compatible and perfect unions in existence, but most married people will have times of struggle and recovery. Blood will be drawn but stanched, stitches will heal, and scars will grow practically invisible. Couples can plod on through deep dark tunnels of mire and limp to reconciliations in the Light. Lazarus-like marriages live after coming forth from the tomb. If not, and the marriage stays dead, then the peace of Christ can still give comfort to hearts that embrace forgiveness. Martyrs from St. Stephen to the present forgive their persecutors, and ex-marital partners can also be magnanimous with the Spirit's help. Benevolent charity and sorrow replace hostility.

Long-lasting marriages that avoid fatality can still suffer from disease, poverty, unemployment, addiction, mental illness, and accidents. External events produce the pressure that opens hidden flaws of character in individuals.

Sometimes, of course, hardships strengthen a union; the couple grow together and jointly surmount misfortune. We can all call to mind the intensely bonded parents of ill children, or hardworking couples who climb out of poverty. Less easy to overcome are the problems arising from internal conflict. The spouse lapses from a common faith, or withdraws from former ideals of work and family, or most hurtful of all, desires a new partner and no longer wants to be married, at least not to you. Rejections and betrayals are all the more bitter if the marriage has been good and fruitful in the past. The greater the height, the greater the fall. Surely oceans of tears have been shed over infidelity and the bitter, bitter betrayals of love. How Christ must have suffered when his friends denied and abandoned him. And how the father of lies rejoices at the deceptions practiced to justify marital infidelity.

For Better

Christian marriage is incredibly supportive in championing the ideal of fidelity and permanent commitment—what people of faith call "covenant love." But how do you become committed to commitment? In my own case as an unchurched child, fairy stories like "The Steadfast Tin

Soldier" and "The Princess and the Goblin" did the job. I was thrilled by the heroic perseverance displayed—all for love, no sacrifice too great, loyalty to the end. After becoming a Christian, I could see that God's faithfulness to the Covenant and the revelation of the Cross had inspired the authors I had read. As adults we can recognize that we aspire to be faithful because God keeps faith with us. At every Eucharist we receive the good news of God's steadfast love. The witness of the Church and our fellow Catholics confirms us. Fidelity and promise keeping are ideals of Western culture that have seeped into our bones. Or at least they used to.

Today, when I talk to young persons about marriage I can draw a blank look when I mention the importance of keeping your promise, of *making* your marriage work, and remaining faithful to the end. One young friend, who after six years of marriage and two children, proceeded to get a divorce, frankly admitted, "Everything was fine, Jim was a wonderful provider, a great father, but I'm just not in love with him anymore." No excuses of abuse, adultery, domestic hate, or mutually assured destruction were offered to justify flight. Unhappiness and boredom were considered enough reason to dissolve the marriage—in hopes of starting over while there was still time.

My encounters with secular approaches to marriage have forced me to delve into my own thoughts on permanent commitment. Do I want to be a curmudgeon who yells out in the crowd, "So what's love and happiness got to do with staying married?" No, definitely not. I am a true believer in romantic love, and am sure that God desires us to be happy. Freud might think romantic love is an illusion in which humans "overvalue the love object," but this seems all wrong from a Christian point of view. God always "overvalues" us, far more than a besotted lover. *Eros* as well as the benevolent charity of *agape* (selfless love) characterizes God's love for us. Every hair on our head is numbered and God is closer to us than we are to ourselves. Our main difficulty lies in not being able to sustain God's erotic loving intensity within marriage. Mothers and fathers seem to do better in their persevering adoration of their infants. The blissful attention given to newborns provides an exemplary model for how we should love the body, mind, and spirit of a spouse. "With my body I thee worship," as spouses used to proclaim in the wedding ceremony.

Sharing ecstatic sexual happiness is the unique gift of marriage. Conjugal joy gives a glimpse of God's joy in loving. The enlivening quality of sexual pleasure rarely receives its due in either the religious or the secular world. Touch communes, consoles, comforts, arouses, and creates a home for married lovers. Sexual joy sustains individuals on the arduous pilgrimage toward unity. Suffering with each other's sorrows is also a part of married life, but mutual joy is primary. For Christians, sexual ecstasy testifies to the Resurrection; ah yes, the good news is not too good to be true, all will be well. Many Americans make an idol of the body and claim sexual satisfaction as an entitlement, but true passion remains suspect to those cautious types who must always be autonomous and cautiously in control. Passion, they say, leads to too much sacrifice and self-forgetfulness.

No, my problems with current secular attitudes toward marriage have little to do with excessive attention to sexuality and romance. Instead, I am offended by the passivity and fatalism displayed. The message I would really like to shout from the rooftops would go like this: "Listen, dearest ones, you are free persons and have the capacity to shape your feelings, your actions, and your marriage. To marry and to love are active verbs." I agree that love should be recognized as a gift, but that does not mean that individuals have nothing to do with engendering love by becoming ready to receive the gift. Individuals are free to direct their attention and act so that love can be born and reborn, again and again. "Falling out of love" sounds like a person is being reduced to an inert object pushed along by determined physical laws. Boredom does not exist as a thing, but lives only in the mind's responses. If you withdraw energy and attention from another and concentrate solely on the self, boredom always follows. To escape the half-life, you must pay attention and throw yourself into the flow. The old maxim, "Do what you're doing," works for everything from sex to conversation to work. Human beings cannot always control what happens to them, but they can freely direct their attention and choose their attitudes. If I do not feel desire, I can desire to desire, and beseech the Lord of Desire to enkindle my heart.

Good marriages, or good-enough marriages or even very successful marriages will not be blissful at every moment. After all, one great task of marriage is to grow up and reach maturity. In the old days we called this painful process "mutual sanctification," but it can also be known as shaping each other up. Since every flaw is magnified in close encounters, confrontation is inevitable in any process of establishing a union. The fights in the American Continental Congress were small potatoes compared to achieving a marital union. And since nothing ever stays the same, marital challenges are perpetually arising and must be negotiated and resolved. The marital conversation goes on forever. And it is not just sex, time, and money—the eternal issues that sociologists point to as occasioning the central conflicts of marriages. More complicated questions of childrearing, career, politics, and religion require mutual decisions. Over many years two people establish their common world through millions of daily interactions and empathic responses. Talking, touching, eating, and sleeping together keep love alive and chaos at bay. Each marriage is a small civilization or oasis at the edge of an indifferent desert. Building up a sturdy edifice—carefully, carefully—takes years. Unfortunately, in a fallen world, marriages, like the great library of Alexandria that took centuries to establish, can be burned down in hours.

Marital happiness and joy are always by-products of other activities. Happiness drops down like dew on the grass when partners work well, serve others, celebrate, worship, pray, and play together. No more psychologically acute words were ever spoken than "it is more blessed to give than to receive." Giving to another expands the sense of self. Through empathy, persons take vicarious pleasure in another's happiness. In the mysterious economy of the Trinity, giving is receiving, loving and being loved increase simultaneously and engender more love. Those who have, receive more.

Love always overflows and creates new things. Good marriages come in many varieties. Despite what Tolstoy said, unhappy families are the ones that are all alike. Love and joy give a freedom to work out many different solutions for combining work and family life. Different temperaments and capacities of two individuals can meld and flourish in many different ways. My husband and I have specialized in the twin marriage in which we are both fairly driven to accomplish intellectual work and publish a lot. Except for an equally prolific family commitment, we lead a life that is mostly work and little play. (With the exception of tennis.) Outsiders may rarely understand other people's operating marital systems, but then they don't have to. The unique language has to be understood only by the natives. Naturally, every unique marital speak is made more idiosyncratic by the use of silences, gestures, looks, and myriad other meaningful signals.

Surely one of the joys of marriage is acting in a long-running soap opera in which you have the leading roles. There's no need to spend time or energy filling in the complicated story line, so the partners can concentrate on the current episode. The running jokes don't have to be explained. Sometimes I am sure that a shared sense of humor and a capacity for wit are the most important requirements for marital success.

Till Death Do Us Part

A long marriage progresses through many different stages and seasons in its own unique style. The young marriage will be filled with opening gambits that give way to more complicated strategies of play. The object is not to win, or to avoid losing, but to create and enjoy an "infinite game."

Only gradually does it become clear that human finitude will force an endgame. Death's ultimate checkmate comes nearer as friends and relatives disappear from the scene. As we approach the marital milestone of fifty years, some good and bad things become clear.

One good comfort of old age is the fact that no one can take your past away from you (short of the curse of Alzheimer's disease). Our five grown sons and a daughter provide companionship and grandchildren. Watching your children's soap operas has its own interest, even if you have been demoted to a minor part. The many books by Callahans upon the shelves provide evidence that two writers live here who have kept on plugging away. Less concrete mementos of the past exist in multiple images of the full press of domestic engagements that filled the years. Who can keep track of all the Christmas dinners, family vacations, party celebrations—or the family emergencies including illness, deaths, accidents, career changes, estrangements, reconciliations, and tuition bills. Is there life after graduate school? No, because after we struggled to get our aptly named "terminal degrees" (nine years each), our grown children enrolled and began their careers. After traumatic adolescent adventures, a period I try to forget, all our children have reached the stable (or sort of stable) civilized status of early middle age.

Chapter 7: On Being a Catholic Spouse

The future, however, does not look rosy. As we look around at contemporaries and those a decade or so older, we cannot avoid the sight of decline and debilitating illnesses. Thank God we have each other "to see us through," as they keep saying in Henry James's novels. My strategy for this next phase is a tried-and-true one: "Take one day at a time." Long ago I aspired to live "the sacrament of the present moment." This focus upon the present works well at every stage of life but is particularly appealing as the days dwindle down to a precious few. Admittedly, there may be only a fine line between living one day at a time and the primitive psychological defense of denial. If so, I'll think about it tomorrow, as Scarlett O'Hara said. Without denial, or letting the troubles of the day be enough thereof, I would never have survived and gotten through so much work and family travail. I had to perfect an ability to put worries out of mind. In fact, if you want to get any writing done, you have to be able to forget about everything else and focus on your assignment. So I am not about to change my defenses or my spiritual aspirations.

When I read the obituaries each morning, I offer a two-second prayer. "Lord, when the moment is upon me, let me commend my spirit in gratitude." Dying must be much like childbirth, so let it be as quick and painless as possible. Why die a thousand deaths ahead of time? Today I choose to throw myself into new projects. More family vacations, more grandchildren visits, more study, more lectures, more yoga, more writing commitments. To this end, I have adopted a new favorite among the consoling psalms. I keep going back to the most promising bits of psalm 92:

> The righteous flourish like the palm tree,
>> and grow like a cedar in Lebanon.
> They are planted in the house of the LORD;
>> they flourish in the courts of our God.
> In old age they still produce fruit;
>> they are always green and full of sap,
> showing that the LORD is upright;
>> he is my rock, and there is
>> no unrighteousness in him (12–15).

Staying green and full of sap means recognizing that life is a comedy rather than a tragedy. Joy and fruitfulness trump sorrow. When you flourish in the house of the Lord, joy is the rock that sustains you. I well remember how in our marriage ceremony we heard that "marriage is the greatest happiness known to man in this vale of tears." In the over-confident arrogance of my twenty-one years, I scoffed at the morbid description of the world as a vale of tears. And I seriously underestimated the importance of happiness. Today I might be less quick to see marriage as distinct from the vale of tears. Being married has become synonymous with being alive. And since life is good, I am ready to affirm that, despite everything, we are meant to live happily ever after.

Questions for Reflection: *What is love? What is "covenant love"? If God is love, three Persons in one Being, how can faith in God help us love one another better? What tools does the Catholic Church offer married couples in handling conflict, maintaining balance, raising children, and living full lives together? In what ways can married life give witness to Christian life? Which marriages do you see as fully expressing God's love? How might even difficulties in marriage bring a couple closer to God?*

Chapter 8

Schooled in the Spirit: On Being a Catholic Teacher

Paul Mariani

I came to teaching early and have never looked back. Sure, there were moments of lunacy when I saw myself decked out in a dark suit and a briefcase in an office on the twenty-third floor of some tower overlooking the lower Hudson, buzzing to have my secretary bring me a cappuccino as I leafed through the latest earnings reports. But then reality filters back in, and I realize that for me, there's always been the one life only.

When I was sixteen, my parents drove me up to Beacon, New York, in the old Plymouth and dropped me off at the high school prep that served to test young vocations to the Marianist Order. I should have been entering my last year at Chaminade High in Mineola, Long Island, but a young priest had suggested I might have a vocation, and wondered if I would be willing to test that vocation at their school sixty miles north of New York City. I would—and did—for a year. Oh, I missed my family. At odd moments I even missed the half dozen girls I was sure were out there somewhere pining for me.

But I loved it at Beacon, among those rolling hills, in the shadow of the mountain that faced us. It was there that I fell in love with God. And with books. Looking through some old letters I wrote my mother back then—in '56 and '57—I see I once actually got a score of 100 in physics. I loved those experiments, and recorded them in sixteen different colors in the pages of my physics notebook. But what I remember most vividly is the little German priest— Fr. George Reich—who taught us fourth-year Latin. Once he showed me his small library, with his hardcover copies of Lucretius and Livy and Virgil and Catullus and Juvenal and so many others. *That*, I decided, was what I wanted to be: a scholar who could open the world of books and pass that knowledge on to others. I saw myself as someone who could walk into a classroom and quip something in Latin, someone who could listen to a two-thousand-year-old ghost summoned to life again because I had the words to do that.

Translate the strange Latin ciphers, and suddenly Dido was whispering to Aeneas again, or Pliny was at Pompeii as Vesuvius erupted on a summer's day. I remember too how Fr. Reich's small frame trembled at the consecration in the little gothic chapel, long ago torn down to make room for a public high school. To be able to consecrate myself to something big and wonderful and mysterious: *that* was something I wanted for myself.

And then, one spring day, while I was serving as goalie on one of our makeshift soccer teams, the image of a young cheerleader began crowding my mind. I remember that moment as if it were happening now. The soccer action was all down at the other end of the field just then, and so there were just the two of us: me and the ghost cheerleader waving her pompoms and doing a little two-step with her feet and hips. And suddenly I found myself promising that, if (or when) I returned home, I would go on to school to become a teacher. If I could not be a priest according to the order of Melchizedek, if I saw my life as a married man, a father with children, then at least let me be found worthy to be a teacher devoted to spending himself in the service of others, and let me work out my life's goal there.

And so it went—with detours here and there—as I sought to expand the possibilities one life can contain. Several images crowd the mind as I write this. One is of Manhattan

College in the fall of 1959, entering the office that served five
or six professors. All laymen at an all-male school, all of them
English teachers, each with his desk and chair and a small
shelf for books. One of them is drinking coffee from a mug
and reading the *New York Times*. A pile of student papers and
some books lie on a corner of the desk. It's only half past nine
in the morning, but already I've driven the thirty miles to college from my home in Mineola and have sat through my first
class of the day.

The night before, I would have worked from six until
ten at an A & P six miles from home for $1.25 an hour,
stocking shelves on the night crew. I am nineteen. How lux-
urious, I think, to be able to read the paper and sip coffee and
then rise to teach Shakespeare or eighteenth-century literature. And I, who even now hardly ever read the papers (except
for six comic strips), decide once again that, yes, that is what
I want to do: read the *New York Times* and make learned and
witty references to world events in my teaching, linking past
with present, to show the whole—life and literature—as one
living fabric.

Nineteen sixty-one. In Plato's Cave over coffee we
watch on a black-and-white TV screen as a young astronaut
named John Glenn, hermetically sealed into a tiny capsule
atop a towering missile out of which white vapors pour,
prepares to become the first American to circle the earth, alas,

months after Yuri Gagarin has already done that in spades. Indeed, President Kennedy has promised that we will put an American on the moon by the end of the decade who will assuredly kick up the lunar dust. It seems imperative to do so.

Back then, the Cold War was palpable in everything we did. Sitting for my graduation photo that fall, I listened to a radio announcing the failed Bay of Pigs invasion, then to JFK's terse remarks taking full responsibility for the fiasco. We were living through important, vital times, and even then we knew it. Even better, I was taking a course of study to prepare myself to understand how we had come—through five millennia—to where we now were as a civilization. So many achievements by so many, even in that pre-computer age in science and art. On the downside, there was the Bomb looming over everything. Instant Armageddon that could strike at any moment.

But there is another image as well—one that goes deeper than the others. It too goes back to Manhattan College. It's an image that informs the others, informs the felt sense of what it means to follow a vocation, and so seems more elusive than the others, elusive in the way that grace is elusive—like air that seems blue but which is transparent, everywhere, and life-sustaining. It's an image of quiet self-giving, the way the Christian brothers in black *soutane* with the funny miniature white twin tablets that served as collars gave of themselves each day to hundreds of young men from working-class Irish, German, Italian, and Hispanic families. Each day, year in and year out, they were there—Brother Paul and Brother Walter and Brother Andrew and Brother Leo. It never occurred to me to ask what their own life stories might have been. They were there to be consulted and used up, by young men hungry for a chance to enter the greater world beyond. In short, they were devoted to what they did, teaching long hours day after day, though it would only strike home years later what secret strengths they must have derived from the Eucharist to keep them going like that, breaking themselves daily like the host for others.

I was like a sponge then, absorbing whatever I could, and always coming back for more. I took 156 credits in the four years I was there. I existed on nervous energy, trying to swallow as much of the universe as I could. I weighed 155 pounds when I entered, and perhaps three pounds more when I graduated. I ate ideas, lived on them, and hungered for more—and after forty years, I still hunger for them. I ingested as best I could not only the subtleties of Scholasticism and the Medieval Philosophers of Light but the significance of the early warning DEW line stretching over northern Canada. I absorbed Egyptian art and Isaiah and Job, along with Sappho and Homer and Aeschylus. Digested the Gospels, Augustine, El Cid, Dante, Luther, Hobbes, Hegel, and Wittgenstein. Ate Shakespeare and Milton and Wordsworth with my daily bread, along with Blake and my beloved Hopkins and the Eliots—George and Tom. Took in Emily Dickinson, Hardy and Stevens and Williams, Bach and Beethoven, Michelangelo and Rembrandt, Cézanne, Braque and Picasso, Marx, Freud, Jefferson, Lenin, Mussolini, Hitler, FDR, and Mao. This and more, all of it arranged in semester units—art, history, philosophy, and literature—from the Sumerians up through the still-fresh mid-twentieth century. All of it was laid out for me by teachers likewise hungry to share what they knew.

I thought then that the course of studies I was pursuing had been in place forever, but it was something far more fragile than that, and within a few years of graduating, the curriculum gave way to other far more fragmented paradigms. Now, having taught college myself for the past forty years, when I see students with so much more choice graduating without an adequate sense of the historical and cultural unities underlying our civilization, I am glad I was given the opportunity I was, and only sorry my own students were not given an equal opportunity.

Of course—like any model—the Grand Tour needed fine-tuning. It had to open itself more to Asian and African and Latin American and feminine realities. But one needed to start somewhere, and where I found myself—as a kid from

New York in the late 1950s—was as good a place to start as any I have found. The proof is that I have ransacked my undergraduate education a thousand times over to make connections with my own specialized field of study, which turned out to be the poetry of the late, great twentieth century. And though so many of the teachers I had then have crossed over the Great Divide to their reward, I thank them often in the silent interstices of the day and night for what they gave me, including the desire and wherewithal to spend my own life teaching students, the vast majority of them from working-class families like myself.

I think of Harry Blair, with his old-world manners, double-breasted suits, paisley ties, and horn rimmed glasses, expounding on the subtleties of metaphysical poetry. Think too of the infinitely gentle John Fandel, who first listened to my tentative sorties into poetry. Of Brother Abdon Lewis, for whom learning and standards were paramount. Of Brother Gabriel, who made Renaissance history so alive one felt one might get off the subway, climb the steps, and suddenly find oneself in Thomas More's London. And of dear Brother Luke, reading galleys for the *Catholic Encyclopedia* in a classroom up in the World War II Quonset huts on the high ground, while we wrote our inadequate and confused summations on the intimate mystery of the Triune God. That too was what I wanted to do someday: write and then scrutinize my own about-to-be-published galleys, blue-penciling my own contributions to the great body of literature.

What was it about, this community of teachers? God knows it was not just the pursuit of knowledge, though I too have pursued that quest my entire life, and expect to go on pursuing it into eternity. As I think of it now, it was something off camera that gave this place its special charism and has endeared it to me in the years since I walked out of those halls to enter the larger world beyond. Call it prayer, call it Eucharist, serving Mass in the main chapel, still in Latin. The invocation to go up to the altar of God, *ad Deum qui laetificat, juventutem meum.* Call it the fuel that kept the dream alive in the long afternoons of moving, elusively, forward. We do move forward, by inches often, and the years go on. And yet, if the truth be told, at the heart of it are the silences and the sacred spaces that nurture and feed us: pregnant silences, world-mothering possibilities.

One October three years ago, I was invited back to Manhattan College to receive an honorary degree. The place was the same, and yet of course different. The trees on the quad were gone, every one of them, and only Brother Luke, of all those who had taught me, still remained from that time thirty-five years before. And yet, even had I not returned, those spaces and those memories would remain locked in the inner sanctum of the heart, where the brothers in black *soutane* are always a jouncy forty or so, as they stride across the quad between classes or on their way to chapel to feed us. Yes, they feed us.

৯৯৯

I think too of my two years at Colgate in the flint-backed ice-green Chenango Valley of upstate New York, where winter seemed always the dominant weather, and remember my teachers there: Joe Slater, who taught the Romantics; Russ Spears, who taught Hardy and Frost; and dapper Bruce Berlind, who taught Renaissance lyric and modern poetry. I think of my first teaching job there—four sections of freshman composition, ten to a class, myself twenty-three and just married and knowing nothing, but giving everything I had, and learning by gulps and gasps, day after day, teaching writing when, with my congenital deafness, I had so very much to learn about the subject itself. I remember one afternoon just before Thanksgiving that year, when a student walked into our basement class-room just as I had finished teaching Hemingway on the art of dying, breaking in to say President Kennedy had been shot. Then climbing the stairs with Mike Begnal, the young Joyce scholar, the two of us wondering how long it would take Kennedy to recover, assuming the incredible rumors were true.

Paul Mariani

I think of Hunter College in midtown Manhattan. The year is 1967. It's the twelfth floor. I'm a doctoral candidate in English at the Graduate Center of the City University of New York. By now Eileen and I have two small sons and a third is on the way. I have just had my first literary essay—it's on Carlyle and the myth of Odin and the death of Christianity—accepted for the university publication. I am to stop at Irving Howe's office and he is to suggest changes and then take care of editing the piece. As I walk past his open door, I see him busy reading galleys, perhaps for *Dissent* of his book on Hardy. He has a blue pencil in his hand, with which he is making corrections on long curved scrolls. He is hunched over his table, for the moment oblivious to the world. And I think, yes, yes again, that is what I want to do. Work over my own writing, revising, polishing myself to a high buff. That, and reveal the deep secrets of *Nostromo, Middlemarch* and *The Golden Bowl* to students as hungry to learn as I am.

I think too of Allen Mandelbaum, master teacher and translator of Dante, Homer, Virgil, and Ovid, as well as of the Italian moderns, Ungaretti, Quasimodo, Montale, and Giudici. He was in his mid-thirties then, fresh from his sojourn in Rome and Florence, and he taught me Dante and modern poetry and so much more—a deep respect for the Word. How shall I ever forget those weekly evening lectures, periods so intense I used to reel home afterwards on the Flushing line, my head feeling as if it might burst with so much new knowledge. Every week a new world opened. How did he do it?

If I modeled my teaching on anyone, it was on this man, though of necessity, being a hopeless monoglot, I learned to put my own idiosyncratic spin on things. I knew I could never duplicate this son of a distinguished rabbinical family, for whom the Text—in Latin, French, German, Hebrew, or Italian—was everything. Besides, when I began teaching in New York, it was police officers at the John Jay College of Criminal Justice, located at the police academy on 23rd Street. Cops and—on the other hand—students at the Bronx campus of Hunter (now Lehmann College), deeply unhappy with our foreign policy. Weirdly, democratically, I taught both groups pretty much the same fare: composition and introduction to literature, learning as much from them as they from me. Frank Serpico out of uniform downtown, and—uptown—Lenin's grandson manqué in the student uniform of the day.

No doubt about it. Back then several of my students were *the* campus radicals. Older students, some of them, which made them almost my age, armed with bullhorns and angry as wasps over Vietnam and the draft. I remember once—how can I ever forget it?—teaching Robert Browning's

"My Last Duchess." I'd researched the libraries for information on Renaissance painting and the nineteenth-century development of the dramatic monologue and was holding forth, when a bearded student stopped me, protesting that the poem was really about the pathological treatment of women by men with the power of life and death. *That's* what Browning was after, he half insisted, half cajoled. And *that* was what was important.

Caught off guard, I demurred. But thinking about it later, I had to admit that what he'd said was most compelling about the poem. In that instant, I realized that that was where my responsibility as a teacher lay: with getting to the heart of the matter. He may as well have added a footnote on the imperial imagination and our policy in Vietnam. Otherwise, the poem was merely historical . . . and dead. But with that core, the poem was as fresh to my students as it had been when Browning had written it a hundred years before. Enjambed couplets and Renaissance Italian history were important, but they were tools only and not the poem. I have never forgotten that moment, though for the love of me I cannot remember the young man's name. Well, I pay that debt here, in these pages, and to so many other students who taught me, while I went on with the fiction that I was teaching them.

The core of the poem, the core of a novel, of an argument, the core of a prayer. The fact that there is meaning, logic, the *logos* at the heart of the matter, something we can know. The fact too that the form of a sentence, a paragraph, a lyric, a story, all tell us something, and that all of these can be ascertained. Knowledge, I have come to see, *can* be imparted. Perhaps not all of it, exactly as we would like, for do we ever really know our own minds totally? But enough of it. A kind of call and counter-response.

The thing is, we're there to educate, to draw out our students, to stretch them, to make them see new possibilities. New thresholds, as Hart Crane says, new anatomies. We're there to serve, to make accessible, to light a fire.

Whenever I can, I try to make daily Mass. It's something I learned the hard way: that the reality of what goes on at Mass in the breaking of the bread, in the breaking of God each day for us, is something I can bring to the class, where I in turn can break myself for those entrusted to me. Of course I've never said this to my students, but there it is anyway: flame divided among ten, twenty, thirty, a hundred, without diminishment. As at the Easter Vigil Mass between the entombment of Holy Saturday and Easter Sunday, where a single flame lights one, then two, then four, then a hundred and a thousand candles, until the darkness is driven back by the Light. Isn't that what teaching does, the teacher feeding the student, students feeding their teacher? Perhaps in that give-and-take we have a hint of how God most intimately works in the Trinity, Creator to Only-Begotten, while the light of the Holy Spirit moves eternally between.

Questions for Reflection: *In what ways does faith spark a hunger for knowledge and a desire to teach? What is the relationship between faith and reason? In what ways does Jesus continue to teach his disciples? How do you continue to learn from the events and people in your life? Why is it important to think about the content of faith, to work toward an examined faith life? What characters in the Bible serve as good models of teachers and students?*

Chapter 9

In the Service of Others: On Being a Catholic Social Worker

Monica Kolb Andrews

March 4, 1993

    As I read through Paolo Freire's chapter from his book
Education Liberation and the Church, *I realized that, according to Freire, a reaction of "neutrality" towards poverty and oppression isn't really a choice at all. Neutrality to Freire means more than just a cold acceptance of the status quo, of complacency and comfort. If that were all, I suppose that I, too, might fall in this category—I am neutral . . . I care about those who are less fortunate, but . . . it really stops there. But for Freire, neutrality implies oppression. If one is not actively engaged against poverty and oppression, then neutrality allows those less fortunate to remain victims. But all this talk of poverty and oppression*

makes me a bit uncomfortable. After all, it is far easier to call myself "neutral" than to consider myself an oppressor. How can I "a woman!" be an oppressor? Perhaps what Freire is saying makes a bit more sense if I take into account that I have gifts, resources, and talents, and then choose only to use them for my own personal gain. If I consciously choose not to use these gifts and talents to help those in need, then neutrality, insofar as it is a conscious choice, becomes oppression.

. . . One of the reasons I decided to participate in the service learning semester abroad program is that I wanted to help others. I had not even considered the possibility that I, too, would be changed in the process, that others would be able to help me in ways that I could not at all foresee. At the same time, I also had a fear that I would come home a changed person. Looking back now, I think I would hate myself if I returned home to Creighton the exact same person I was before I left. There is something deep inside me that wants to be part of something bigger, that wants to make changes in the world, and that wants to be changed from being "neutral" to something much more.

This passage is taken from a journal I kept while participating in a service learning semester abroad during my junior year at Creighton University. I had heard about the program quite by accident, and decided to attend an hour-long information meeting one night as a way of procrastinating having to prepare for a biology exam. Pictures of white, sandy beaches and romantic thoughts of warm, Caribbean nights soon flooded my imagination. Little did I conceive how God was somewhere behind these quiet proddings in my heart, and even less could I imagine then how life-changing this experience of "helping others" would be for me. As I look back on my experience in the Dominican Republic from an eight-year's hindsight, I see now how it laid the foundation for my chosen career path as a social worker and, even more, helped introduce me to a whole new way of learning to live my faith. My experience living abroad provided me with a whole new understanding of Catholic social teaching, an appreciation that continues to influence my life, faith, and work, sometimes in very surprising ways.

Today I am a social worker in a Cystic Fibrosis (CF) center at a local hospital. My position offers me the opportunity to work with children, adolescents, young adults, and their families as they try to manage the daily impact of living with such a devastating chronic illness. My role in both the inpatient and outpatient hospital settings is multifaceted. I assess the functioning capacity of the patient and any family members directly related to the illness. More often than not, this means providing a psychosocial assessment of the familial level of functioning as well as the various levels of care. Also, I assist families in developing and implementing plans for continued home services and other needs in the larger community. This might include counseling patients and families on how to make adjustments to changing levels of illness, strengthening family and care-giver capacities, and even helping eliminate any physical, mental health, safety, or welfare barriers that might prevent the patient and his or her family from reaching a maximum level of healthy, interpersonal, and individual functioning.

My role varies with each family's specific needs. Most important though, as a social worker I am trained to put myself "in the shoes" of the patient or family. In empathizing with those who are living with a chronic illness, I am forced to look at the reality of their everyday struggles. Many of the kids wake up at 5 A.M. each morning. And rather than jumping into their parent's bed or taking it easy, they begin their day with a nebulizer treatment, then undergo a half an hour of chest-physical therapy only to repeat the same cycle later in the evening. Their days are filled with the constant struggle to gain or maintain their weight as well as taking enzymes to help their body digest their food intake. Their lives, although normal, are challenged and impacted every day by the need to care for their body, especially their lungs. I am often reminded of how Jesus chose to comfort those who suffered in similar ways. For many, the challenge of living with cystic fibrosis is met with courage and perseverance. Others struggle to find answers to questions such as, Why me? When am I going to die? Or why bother when I am eventually going to die from CF anyway? To minister to this population is to walk with them as they struggle to find meaning and hope in their lives.

The opportunity to share with the patients and their families allows me to become a companion and source of support for them and their loved ones. I have been especially touched working with patients and their families who are confronting end-of-life issues. As you can imagine, assisting someone to prepare for the inevitability of death is not a happy task, but it is a powerful reminder to me of how beautiful, strong, and vulnerable each person is. I find that in supporting patients and their families in the process of accepting and anticipating grief, I have myself become more connected to my own experiences of loss and a deeper sense of the Christian meaning of hope.

My work with cystic fibrosis has been both rewarding and difficult. Often, I am reminded of my own mortality. In recent months I have been working closely with a young adult who now finds himself at a point where his lungs are severely deteriorated. For him, hope lies in the possibility of a lung transplant that could prolong his life, though the reality is that the process is long and filled with many uncertainties. Our work together has helped this patient prioritize his needs and wants, discuss and evaluate his treatment options, as well as be open about his fears, hopes, and dreams for the future. My role to offer support, education, and encouragement has helped this patient in accepting his position and moving forward in acceptance of his future.

I have also been able to connect with a young girl who has severe health issues, but who is now faced with limited medical options to help sustain her life. At the same time, I am working with her family on how to deal with their own grief and sadness in trying to learn how to accept the unacceptable. I assist the family, whose only desire is to comfort their daughter, to articulate their hopes and desires as they help their daughter prepare to die. I have often found that sometimes my presence is the only gift that I can give—and at times it seems the most appropriate intervention.

My role in the Cystic Fibrosis Center is directly connected with my faith, in that I support and assist patients and families to bring issues to the table that may be difficult, but that make life, preparing for death, death itself, and life after death more fulfilling experiences. I learn from families every day about the courageous ways patients and their brothers, sisters, moms, dads, other family members, and friends deal with the effects of living and dying from a terminal illness like cystic fibrosis. Their courageous faith impacts how I live my life. Through prayer and reflection, I try to find solace in those difficult yet graced moments when I can be with these families in their time of need. Illness and death are not frightening to me; my faith enables me to find a sense of peace in all of the suffering I encounter. Moreover, my ministry to others helps me to assist families to attain their own comfort and hope.

A few years ago, while studying in graduate school for my master's degree in social work, I participated in a year-long internship at an AIDS service organization. My role was to help clients access necessary resources as well as to provide supportive counseling. My position as a case manager both challenged and strengthened my faith. Many of the clients receiving services at the agency were not only infected with a devastating virus, but they also faced a stigma placed upon them by society. One of the reasons I believe I was called to work with this population is because to me they represent the modern-day outcast, the oppressed or the leper that Jesus would want to reach out to with compassion, while others watch on the sidelines with shock, disdain, or even silent contempt. This sense of compassion is what I tried to offer to my clients.

Compassion or empathy is a core principle in establishing a healthy therapeutic relationship with a client. Moreover, as a social worker I focus on being where the client is in what the popular lingo calls "the here and now." To me, this represents an almost spiritual or sacred place to share with another person. I worked with one client whom I will call "James." James had struggled to find his place in society as well as the acceptance of his own sexuality as a gay man. In our many conversations, James would often talk about how he felt terribly alone, ashamed, and even dirty because he was "diseased." I worked with James for about a year. As our relationship came to a close, James shared with me that he didn't think anyone could love and respect him because he was HIV positive, but that our relationship had challenged his beliefs about himself entirely. He had internalized society's views of what it means to be a gay man infected with HIV, and he had lived that way ever since he was first diagnosed eight years earlier.

Our conversations together allowed James to experience his own humanity for the first time. He discovered within himself what God had desired for him all along: to celebrate the gift of his life and to allow someone to love him as he is, a human being infected with a virus. As the end of my internship approached, James was able to share his diagnosis with many of his family and friends. Although this was a very scary process for him, James realized that he was able to find the respect, love, and support that he so much desired from those who loved him the most, and that was because he learned to respect, love, and support himself.

My work with James allowed me to experience God's grace in new and surprising ways. As a social worker, I have experienced the empathic-helping relationship as a reflection of love and a tangible presence of God's self-gift in Jesus' own ministry to the poor and outcast. Furthermore, the empathic relationship recognizes and reinforces my own Christian faith in human dignity, in the distinctiveness of every human person who stands before God, and the inviolable capacity to choose to remain open to God's grace. My experience with James brought me closer to God and gave me a deeper understanding of the cross and resurrection.

§ § §

As I look back to the roots of my journey, I am again reminded of my semester abroad in the Dominican Republic. As part of the service learning program, I participated in an ongoing community service project. I chose to live in a *campo* or countryside setting with a family on weekends. My project was to educate the community on the importance of protecting the ground water by painting a mural of the water cycle in the local school house. I stayed with the Molina family; Mr. and Mrs. Molina and their four children. They were always warm and welcoming. I can remember sitting at their table with candles for light as they taught me basic words in

Spanish. Their bathroom was a simple latrine and the shower, rainwater. I was amazed at how this family welcomed me into their home and their lives. They were very proud of their simple home, family, and community.

One weekend, about a month into the program, I planned to spend the weekend with the Molina family. I was scared and reluctant to again take a bus and a motorcycle followed by an hour hike to get to their home. Feeling somewhat sick, I sent a message with someone heading to the *campo* that I would not be going that weekend. Through much prayer and thought, I finally realized I was scared of how my experience with the Molina family was already beginning to change me. It was difficult for me to reconcile how I had so much material wealth and this family had so little. I felt guilty for how I lived my life and how material items had gotten in the way of who I really was. The next day I was able to push my fears aside and make the long journey to their home. For me, this was a commitment to God's challenge to learn more about myself by knowing and experiencing life with the Molina family.

I know now that my experience living with the Molinas led me to see the superficiality of my own lifestyle. Through much thought and reflection, I learned how my own desires to experience God in my life had been clouded. I struggled to make clear how I could balance my own needs with my relationship with God and my faith, and how I could simplify my life so I could respond to God's call for me to serve those in need.

I am amazed at how my semester abroad in the Dominican Republic changed my life and faith forever. Moreover, it strengthened my commitment to help others in my day-to-day life as a professional social worker. Today I am inspired to help others through their struggles in life just as I manage mine. As a social worker, I try to be a reminder of God's presence in the lives of my clients by supporting their emotional needs through counseling, as in my relationship with James, or by helping them access necessary community resources to enhance their quality of life. Through my work, I am reminded of God's call in the Bible to know and minister to the poor and suffering. It is, as theologian Paolo Freire wrote, "a permanent challenge to which I must respond."

Questions for Reflection: *When have you been helped by someone else when you were in need? When have you helped another in dire need? What feeling, thoughts, emotions did you experience in each case? What did your experiences teach you about life, love, compassion, suffering? In what ways have your experiences impacted your faith? And how has your faith impacted your desire and ability to serve others? What opportunities to work with the poor do you have in your own life?*

Chapter 10

Beginning in Awe: On Being a Catholic Parent

Tom McGrath

To explain how my experience as parent has been a spiritual path, I have to begin seven years before my first child was born. At age twenty-two, I was feeling more lost in my life than I've ever been before or since. My life was devoid of meaning and more than grim. In my lowest moment, I latched onto one bit of Jesus' teaching that I'd learned in Catholic schools, and I clutched it as if it were a life raft in a storm-tossed sea. The teaching: "Love one another as I have loved you."

With that as my guiding principle, I signed on to work as activities counselor at an orphanage for kids who were wards of the state. I suspect I turned to the work hoping for some kind of escape, but instead I came face to snot-nosed face with life in the form of sixteen five- to nine-year-olds. What I found was a life that could have gone either way—drudgery or joy. On any given day the job provided good amounts of both. But in the course of my time served, I learned that one of the best ways to become a better human being is to find yourself in charge of youngsters who need your love, attention, and steady care.

I was blessed with work so relentless and demanding that I had to forget myself, at least for periods at a time, and simply pour out my energy for others. My *ennui* evaporated in the face of games to be organized, marshmallows to be doled out, and scraped shins and tender hearts to be soothed. These kids relied on me. It was abundantly clear I wasn't perfect at the job, but the boys forgave me my imperfections and went right ahead needing me. Over time I came to know just how much I needed them.

Forgetting myself and willingly caring for the basic bodily and spiritual needs of others reduced life to its essence, and reminded me of what I was so busy trying to forget—my own human vulnerability and need. And of course, when it comes to spiritual growth, accepting one's vulnerability is where it all begins.

And so I was somewhat prepared that being a parent would *demand* a lot from my faith, as well as *do* a lot for my faith. But I never expected fatherhood to be such a radical experience.

ᔆ ᔆ ᔆ

Being a parent begins in awe. And awe, which is akin to fear of the Lord, is a religious experience, one of the gifts of the Holy Spirit. Even the most jaded and cynical new parent, it seems, is not immune to the miraculous nature of birth witnessed up close. Our defenses give way to awe.

Each of my daughters' births was an invitation to a new consciousness. These events confronted me with a truth I had previously overlooked or forgotten: that we are all miracles, products of life's incessant desire to bring forth more life. It was God, the Creator, pulling off yet another glorious encore. Standing so close to this miracle irrupting into the world changes everything forever.

It seemed like much more than coincidence that Stevie Wonder's song "Isn't She Lovely?" was playing over the hospital's Muzak system when I first held my older daughter, moments after her birth on the first day of summer, the longest and brightest day of the year in 1979. Holding her, I knew that my life and identity had changed forever, even unto eternity. She and I were now linked as father and daughter, always and everywhere. This overwhelmed me and redefined me. It called me to a new consciousness and a whole new set of challenges. Holding her in my arms, I realized how totally helpless she was and how dependent she would continue to be for years to come. I kept thinking, "When do I get off duty? Shouldn't there be someone else in charge? Someone who knows what they're doing? God, help!" And so, after awe, my second response to parenthood was prayer.

Awe and prayer: two great ways to energize your faith. They are both invitations to a transformed awareness. Awe lets you know that there are truths in life to reckon with, realities worth paying attention to—like tenderness, commitment, honor, and care, plus an aching, fierce love. And I've learned that prayer has been a ready companion during every age and stage I have accompanied my children through. My struggles as a parent give me plenty to pray for, and my children's lives give me plenty to pray about.

My faith and my work as parent are tightly interwoven. It's hard to tease out where exactly my faith feeds my family life or vice versa. When it comes to family, not much is neat and tidy. As Barbara Coloroso, author of *Kids Are Worth It!* says, "Parenting is an inefficient vocation." It's much more about mystery than mastery. But over time, certain lessons have become clear. Here are a few:

Family life regularly reveals the patterns of Jesus' life, death, and resurrection. This cycle is not just a piece of historical data about Jesus, but is the seed of truth at the heart of Jesus' message. We call it the paschal mystery.

In family life this pattern of dying and rising shows itself early. We see it in the twin parental disciplines of welcoming and letting go, which begin long before the child is even born. When the desire to conceive a new life comes into focus, the couple dies to its old life and becomes willing to disrupt their lives in ways they cannot even yet imagine—all in order to take on the holy work of caring for another human being.

My wife and I remember fondly how our first years of childless marriage were relatively carefree, how we'd work long hours all week and meet at a local pizza joint on Friday nights to catch up over drinks and dinner, and then enjoy an uninterrupted romantic night at home. To everything there is a season, and the season of being married and childless was a good one. But we had to let that one pass away in order to enter fully into the season of making room for children in our life. Being a parent begins with welcoming, with making room. We create a space for them in our home or apartment, but also in our lives. We give up that den where we were going to write the great American novel, or the home office where we can "finally get organized." Instead, we buy

Winnie-the-Pooh lamps, Bert-and-Ernie bedsheets, and a Toy Story mobile. We shift our budget and cut back on our extra-curricular activities in order to be present and available. Eventually we realize (and our childless friends do, too) that it will be years before we can complete an adult conversation without interruption.

We welcome our child's new abilities and independence (the day you can stow the diaper bag permanently stands as a monumental day in most parents' lives), and yet those new capabilities mean we also loosen our controls. Soon they're playing down the block, then crossing the busy street, then going on overnights at friends' homes, off on dates, and the next thing you know you're dropping them off at college or watching them leave for their full-time work. Navigating these changes takes faith and trust. Parents do a lot of praying the first day their child drives off, new driver's license in hand, to round up his or her friends to go who-knows-where.

Parental welcoming and letting go extends to our children's personalities as well. At our best, we welcome who they are rather than whom we want them to be. The Ph.D. mom learns to welcome the daughter whose highest aspiration is to follow in the latest pop star's footsteps. The sports-loving dad discovers his son has a passion for science and wouldn't know Sammy Sosa from Knute Rockne. When we can die to our expectations (especially those we didn't realize we had), we are able to rise to the new and glorious life that awaits us in truth.

And we often need to die to our own traits that get in the way of being the parent we want to be. For some, this means nurturing the patience, consistency, or stability they never believed they had. For others it might include facing up to a debilitating addiction (to drugs, alcohol, work, worry) they'd rather believe "isn't hurting anyone." Family life is loaded with instances of dying and rising to new life. Practicing my faith helps me look at my life and see not just aggravation but opportunity. Not just burden but grace.

Being a parent means you live in community. A while back I visited a friend who is a Trappistine monk. She lives in cloistered community with two dozen other religious sisters who all get up before dawn for morning prayer. They spend their day in prayer, meditation, and doing their share of mundane chores. I asked her what she found the most spiritually challenging aspect of her life in the monastery. She laughed as she responded, "The annoying personality traits of my fellow monks." To which I replied, "I hear ya!"

Living in a house with four adults and one bathroom means that I get up early, and sometimes my day begins by praying mightily that my turn at the facilities will come quickly. We have our chores. We have our chairs at the kitchen table. We have our times of daily prayer and our times of silence, occasionally preceded by a slammed door. And we certainly each have our annoying personality traits that outsiders might find charming but don't wear so well day after day.

The communal nature of family life is a spiritual opportunity. People used to ask an acquaintance of mine how it turned out her family was so close. She always replied, truthfully, "We live in a small house." There was no getting away from one another. That can breed contempt, or it can promote intimacy and care. My faith gives me tools—humility, forgiveness (given and received), respect for the dignity of each individual, patience, and even a sense of humor—to navigate the straits of family life with a certain amount of grace. Each member of the family brings gifts to the table. My daughter Judy can get us all acting silly. Patti delivers the most deliciously wicked one-liners. My wife delights in keeping our lives smoothly organized. And I bring an optimism to the mix. We have friends who regularly fill our house with laughter, compassion, openness, risk-taking, and countless other gifts. Through our commitment to remaining a community of care over time, we create a safe, yet challenging, home base from which we can live the gospel. We feel supported to live lives in which our faith, morals, and values guide our days.

As a Catholic, I also know that my family is merely one community within many other larger communities, including our parish, our neighborhood, society, and the Church around the world. We're even part of the communion of saints who witness to a way of living and a set of beliefs that give our lives meaning. On our own, it would be easier to let these values slide away. Living in a community that lives and worships and plays and prays together, I'm strengthened and emboldened to follow Jesus' way.

Being a parent cuts through your illusions. Having kids guarantees you'll receive regular feedback you'll get nowhere else. I flinched while watching the hilarious Steve Martin rendition of the film *Father of the Bride*, especially that moment where his daughter describes her new fiancé as "just like Daddy, only brilliant." Ouch! A friend told me her fourteen-year-old sternly instructed her one afternoon, "Now when we get to the mall, just pretend we don't know each other."

This may be painful, but it's a great spiritual opportunity. I want my own kids to be impervious to peer pressure, which means to be no slave to others' fleeting opinions of you. We all have our conceits. We use impressive portions of our imaginations in our need to portray ourselves as the hero of our own narrative. When our kids burst our ego-inflated bubbles, the good news is that, underneath it all, they still love us madly. I can drive them nuts with my crazy theories of the cosmos, they still love my pancakes. I can make them goofy with my worries about how they're going to get to their friends' houses and where they're going to park, and yet they still love my stories and my jokes. In fact, like Mr. Rogers, they like me just the way I am. And when you come home from a tough day of office politics and dealing with the public, it can be refreshing to find a welcome that sees through the delusions and loves you anyway.

And as a parent, I relish the opportunity to respond in kind, to let them try on their various personalities and styles, and to be the one who can see through it all to the precious and unique person shining through. At its best, family is the original come-as-you-are party.

Being a parent offers opportunities to perform the corporal and spiritual works of mercy.

When Jesus was asked who would qualify for heaven (see Matthew 25:31–46), he tells them, "Those who feed the hungry, give drink to the thirsty, clothe the naked, and shelter the homeless." These are the stuff of daily family life. Parents do this all the time!

These mundane activities, along with admonitions to visit the imprisoned and bury the dead have been combined into the seven corporal works of mercy that the Church enjoins us to practice as living signs of our faith. I remember the first time I heard this gospel reading with the ears of a parent. Prior to that time I'd always thought I would have to go off to a foreign land and work in some sort of mission in order to live out these teachings. But lo and behold, that very morning I had served my older daughter yogurt and fed a bottle to the baby. My wife and I had struggled to get them into church-appropriate clothes, and off to church we went. During Mass I thought about the work I do to keep a roof over our heads (and to afford enough extra to contribute to our parish's food pantry and take our turn making meals for the homeless shelter). What a joy it was to realize that my life as a parent offers me the very content Jesus pointed to as the way to eternal life. In church that morning, the readings helped me recognize these mundane activities not as burdens and drudgery but as occasions of grace. Sometimes I rise to the occasion. When I worship on Sunday and the celebrant asks God to accept these gifts, the fruit of the vine and the work of human hands, I have plenty to put on the altar— every mundane chore I've accomplished in the previous week as well as all my hopes and concerns for the week to come.

Parents not only feed the hungry, they know the hungry child's favorite kind of pickles. They not only give drink to the thirsty, but they deliver it in a favorite Winnie-the-Pooh cup. We clothe the naked (sometimes we want to follow author Barbara Coloroso's lead and have our kids wear a pin saying "I dressed myself!"), shelter them (and sometimes their lost friends), tend to them when they're sick, help them out of prisons, whether literal or emotional, and we show them what to do and what we believe when it is time to bury the dead. Sometimes, tragically, we have the unspeakably horrible task of burying our own children.

Perhaps more than anywhere else, this is where my faith most informs my work as a parent. This is where I get glimpses of God. "When did we see you hungry, Lord, and feed you?" We see Christ in the need, in the hunger. And when we respond to it with generosity of heart, we nourish not only our children and ourselves, but we nourish Christ in our midst.

§ § §

I asked my wife, Kathleen, what element of her faith supports her work as parent, and without a moment's hesitation she replied, "Romans 8:28." This is her bedrock passage. I remember her reading it with power at her father's funeral years ago before we were married. "For to those who love God, who are called according to his plan, all things work out for the good." And she's been a mother long enough to realize that practicing the faith does not mean that "all things working out for the good" will immunize her family from the slings and arrows of outrageous fortune. Bad things happen even to people we love and pray for. But the passage points to faith at a deeper level, the kind of faith that provides the necessary courage to launch our children into life. Practice of our faith in good times and bad has shown us that there's a God who loves us and abides with us even though we may travel through the valley of death.

In the end, I don't see my role as my kids' "first teacher of the faith" to be yet another developmental chore to check off—like seeing they get art lessons and music lessons or braces when they need them. I have hoped to raise my children immersed in a hearty broth of faith because God is our origin and our destiny, and it would be terribly sad for them to go through life unaware that they are, in Thomas Merton's words, shining like the sun. I saw them shining that way the day they were born. I want them never to forget that.

Questions for Reflection: *Why has the Catholic tradition considered the family to be one of the most important forms of community? What other forms of community nourish your faith? What can we learn from the example of the Holy Family of Mary, Joseph, and Jesus? How do our children show us the loving face of God? What responsibilities and challenges, joys and sorrows are part of community life? How can faith play a part in helping individuals and communities reach their full potential? What does it mean to love others as Jesus loves us? Why is it important to care for and nurture the physical and spiritual growth of children?*

Chapter 11

Acting in Faith: On Being a Catholic Actress

Mimi Kennedy

I'm sure I'm Actress enough to write on this subject. I'm not sure I'm Catholic enough. I suspect many of my fellow Catholics are also uncertain about whether the Vatican Curia would endorse their level of orthodoxy. But I am a Catholic actress, as long as I don't have to apply for a *mandatum*.

I lost my acting career temporarily—it felt permanent then—when motherhood and marriage to my overworked high school English teacher husband swamped my efforts to be effective and attractive at auditions. At the time I phoned a nun friend, Sister Mary Petrus (*née* Sullivan) and sobbed to her that the Catholic Church's delusional ideals of women, marriage, and motherhood cruelly mocked my reality, and I wanted to speak out. She said, "If you're going to take on the Catholic Church, you'd better be mentally healthy." That was seventeen years ago. A brilliant therapist who wasn't afraid to say the words "Holy Spirit" helped me get mentally healthy enough to write about my faith. But an utterly lucid context escapes me. For now, I rely on a few categories to present my thoughts.

Struggles

It's probably best for me to state up front that I struggle— who doesn't?—with faith. I stopped being an obedient daughter of the Church when I recognized that scrupulous obedience induced in me a girlish psychology that wreaks havoc on my life as wife and mother. I was trading obedience for being taken care of when it was time to grow up and care for others. My Catholic conscience insists I confess, here, that my husband and I have, after long hours of prayer and discernment, practiced artificial contraception throughout our marriage. For us, "openness to life" means *nurturing* life, not just remaining "open to reproduction." Lives are not little artworks to fill an empty planet. Life requires tremendous, *ongoing* openness, and the planet is teeming with it! I suffer from knowing that, according to official teaching, conceiving as many of my own children as my conjugal life will allow and accepting the mistakes of "natural" planning would remove sin from our marriage. But my husband and I found that nurturing the lives we've already become part of—our children's, each other's, the school where he teaches and the children learn, my creative community, our political, social, and faith communities—require that we limit our own reproduction while remaining open to the intimacy that keeps our marriage alive and meeting these demands. I practice yoga as prayer, though Pope John Paul II warned against it as too focused on the body. Precisely because my life is so intensely physical, as a mother and actress, I find body-prayer helpful. And I admit that I do not always attend Sunday Mass. When my children were young, I tried, but I would find myself screaming, Sundays after Mass, as my mother had before me. I realized that the calm oasis of Church made me long for girlhood again, which meant wishing my family away. When we began going on hikes or visiting the zoo on Sundays for a while instead of church, our family life improved. My children still find God in nature. For years, they feared church, because they associated it with family arguments and tremendous anxiety, but they've begun, as older teens, to appreciate attending Mass occasionally. I did not do that part of my religion well. I realize now that my problems had a lot to do with the times, and a pastor who told me—when, inspired by my own need, I offered to start a babysitting course whose graduates could babysit free as parish community service—"I'm not sure that babysitting can be considered community service." He idealized marriage, but failed to grasp one of the simplest ways to help struggling couples sustain theirs. Today, that parish is child-friendly, full of families. I like to think I was a harbinger. The truth is, all Catholics struggle with the Church, laypeople and clergy. We must. Otherwise we, and the Church, wouldn't grow.

Religious Identity

Identity is an actor's business. We adopt and drop identities continually as we play different roles. If we become famous, our personal identities become public business. Touting my own religious identity doesn't seem entirely helpful right now; the world is mired in violence in the name of dueling religions. I find nothing godly about making people of other faiths feel their religion is mistaken or inadequate to praise God and save their souls. I am eager, at present, to live my Catholicism "subversively," to let it be an underground spring feeding my life so that it can bear fruit on every branch, not just the "religious" one. I aspire to what St. Paul recommended: unceasing prayer.

And I wonder if that's possible, for an actress.

Conscience

I'm known mostly as a comic actress. At present, I sit in the dressing room of my television sitcom, surrounded by barricades and security guards, meditating on the tragedy of September 11, 2001. People are crying out for justice and meaning, weary of the distractions and greed of materialism. And the world in which I work—Hollywood—is a big part of those distractions. If I'm part of the problem, how can I be part of the solution? If I can't be, my vocation needs to change. Jesus said, "Blessed are they who hunger and thirst for justice's sake, for they shall be satisfied." But He also said the wheat would grow up with the chaff. And Yahweh said, "Vengeance is mine."

I can't fully see the ledger of human history, but I can see my own ledger, and examine my own sins of omission and commission. I am a Catholic actress doing an examination of conscience between visits to the makeup room and calls to my agent. I ask myself, Is being an actress fiddling while Rome burns? Can the money I earn from paymasters, who definitely earned much of it by glorifying the seven deadly sins, do anything worthwhile, laundered by good intention? I try to choose projects that heal or instruct, but isn't my very presence on television, or in movies, an invitation—in many places in the world—to envy, anger, or despair? (Scandal will come into the world, but woe to those by whom it comes.) The gut-wrenching physical fear I feel in a formerly carefree workplace that now faces "unsubstantiated threat" might be a type of justice, I realize. Many in the worldwide audience whom I seek to entertain have lived constantly under this kind of threat. I rarely thought of that. I do now.

Gratitude

My Catholicism gives me many resources to combat fear, and I employ them. There is prayer: the rosary, the Mass. There are the sacraments. There is the examination of conscience, and the whole concept of penance, making voluntary sacrifices. Well-meaning friends have told me, lovingly, over the years, that they fear I dwell on the negative too much. They usually mean I think too much about the suffering in the world. For me, one of the great strengths of Catholicism is its teaching that suffering is a natural part of being human, not a judgment or a mark of shame. Jesus suffered! Suffering and guilt are instructive. By changing us, they help us change the world. I am grateful for a Church whose parochial schools offered theological and moral questions to me and my classmates, often and early. The *Baltimore Catechism* was my first memorized text, and it taught me there *were* answers to the search for human meaning, and I should expect them. Not to expect them was amoral. To question one's answers, eventually, is necessary, but one must have the answers to question. I am now a student of nonviolence, and I often hear the aphorisms, "Evil is the absence of good" and "Evil occurs when good people do nothing." I think of, and am grateful for, the corporal and spiritual acts of mercy, and all the other proscriptions in the catechism that answered the question, What can one individual do against evil?

I'm grateful to the Second Vatican Council for changing some of the hurtful pedagogy I grew up with. I still have nightmares about the hell conjured by grade-school nuns to control unruly children in overcrowded classrooms of sixty or more. I'm sure some of them joined religious orders to escape children and family life; their mental health and ours was put at risk in the name of obedience when they were ordered to teach at age levels to which their skills were not suited. Just in time, Vatican II revealed the nuns' humanity to me—along with their hair, when they abandoned their cellulose wimples. The faithfulness of those Sisters of Mercy inspires me to this day: they embraced change with humility and humor, letting go of their own cultural preferences as their considerable sacrifice, when the Church leapt forward in faith and let the Holy Spirit renew the face of the earth.

Morality

Being a Catholic actress means paying attention to the morality of my work. This has nothing to do with the morality of characters I play—saints or sinners—or even how well I play them, though presenting a character's full humanity always enhances the morality of a story. My moral decisions reside in choice of projects: what I work on, and why. My discernment is flawed and subjective, but I apply it. The pressure to accept any job, when 95 percent of Screen Actors Guild members are out of work at any given time, is enormous. The pressure to accept the highest-paying jobs, when other people—agents, lawyers, accountants, stylists, publicists—depend on your career for their livelihoods, is also great. But as an American television actress, I must consider the effect of my work on the community-at-large—the audience. That community has become very large: it's global.

When I was sent the script for the feature film *Natural Born Killers*, my agent was thrilled to have garnered an audition for me. He described the project as "a satire on America's love affair with violence." Satire? The script was a valentine to violence! I wanted no part of it. My character died horribly at the hands of her maniacally deranged daughter; that was not an image I wanted to leave on film for my own daughter to see someday. "It's an A-project!" my disgusted agent cried when I declined my audition. "And I'm supposed to say now you won't even come in?"

I was proud to do a television project, far less prestigious by industry standards, that was a true story involving medical ethics in premature births. I played a mother in *Baby Girl Scott*, in which a child was profoundly damaged by mandated neonatal intervention. My cousin Tim and his pregnant wife saw the movie a month before their daughter was born with minimal brain function. Tim called me from the hospital for help, asking if, in the course of making the movie, I'd met anyone who could help them make their decisions. They were anguished. I did put them in touch with people who, he said, helped them enormously in making the short weeks of Elinore's life more peaceful.

The impact of that minor role on my family's well-being was instructive; I realized everything I act in has impact. I may never know it, but I must try to imagine it. To pretend there will be no impact can be not modest but self-serving and immoral.

I played a wealthy American wife in *Homefront*, a dramatic series about life in post-World War II Ohio. The writers and I collaborated to make the character's racism, materialism, greed, and narcissism insidiously "normal" and *almost* attractive. But the Woman You Love to Hate isn't just endearingly flawed. Private sins destroy good people by perpetuating public injustice and creating social tragedy. That's an important history lesson we must not repeat. People stop me, ten years later, to mourn *Homefront*'s cancellation.

Dharma and Greg was a pilot script that celebrated love, contrasting country-club conservatism with the old hippie ethic, "Make Love, Not War." I embraced it, and my earth-mother Abby character, and fans have embraced *me* on the street saying, "I wish you were *my* mom." A Japanese girl wrote, "This show makes me love even more my own family." And a woman my own age once said in the supermarket, "Your show makes me feel I can just be myself, without buying into all this *stuff* they're trying to sell us." I applauded her, joking, "Don't tell our sponsors." I'm proud to be part of a story that suggests joy and self-worth come not from things, but from creatively nurturing life with our hearts, hands, and imaginations. That *will* permanently fill the emptiness that savvy marketers understand and exploit!

In my periods of unemployment, I am anxious, like everyone else. But my Catholic conscience helped me see, early on, that my soul was the center to which the jobs attached, not the reverse. It's difficult, because my roles take over, once I'm in them. But letting go, when I'm done, teaches the detachment that Eastern mystics say is crucial for the soul's growth and self-understanding.

Sacrifice

After I became a mother, I turned down many projects because I saw they harmed children or society's attitude towards children. Even scripts I would have considered innocuous became objectionable to my heightened sensitivities. I was offered a lot of mother roles in stories about demon-children and ribald teenagers. I didn't work for a while.

This was in the period when I regularly attended Sunday Mass, with my babies. I needed the Church's consolation for my little ego-losses: I'd been on the cover of *TV Guide* before pregnancy. Now I'd lost all glamour. Yet I was the parish's Catholic Actress, as Loretta Young and Anne Blythe had been *their* parishes' Catholic Actresses. My mother had told me about them after reading movie magazines at the hairdressers, and had been so happy to have Catholic role models for her star-struck young daughter. I was ashamed when I heard congregants whisper disapprovingly as I passed in the communion line: "I'd never have recognized her!" I was clearly letting them down. I went to the pastor for spiritual guidance with the conflicts of motherhood, family, career, and spiritual growth. He asked where my husband was, and suggested therapy. I went—it was a good suggestion—but I was always sorry my faith didn't have more to say to me. The pastor sermonized often about television and movies, and later hosted a lavish celebrity funeral for a famous comedienne whom most people were surprised to learn had been Catholic, because we'd never seen her in church. Clearly he was entranced by showbiz, and the fact that I wasn't, even after being on the cover of *TV Guide*, was for him a sign of mental unbalance.

Catholics believe in marriage-for-life. Actresses often don't. My husband is a high school English teacher, and staying married has demanded split personalities of each of us. We must live in the world of books, teenagers, school activities, hours of reading, and piles of paper to grade in whatever time is "free"—and in Hollywood. His vocation has kept us young and grounded; mine has provided imagination and glamour—which marriages sorely need. I doubt we would have survived with just a civil and emotional contract. But he converted to Catholicism before our wedding. We remember vividly our Nuptial Mass, and we believe our marriage is a sacrament. Though many times I've felt, as married career women inevitably will, that marriage prevented me from achieving what I truly deserved, I know that without our marriage, my husband and I would experience spiritual amputation. Our marriage has become a most important channel for God's grace and joy in our lives. I hasten to add that I believe it's my husband's Methodist upbringing that gives our union a strong foundation in social justice. His childhood congregation was steeped in community action. Though surrounded by inspiring Catholic activists now, I recall the Church of my childhood as more eager to baptize the poor than help them analyze, and change, their social condition.

Community

Catholics believe in the communion of saints. My fellow actors are one of my profession's great joys. There's no people like show people, as the song says. We are attractive and lovable—in spite of, or perhaps because of, our enormous egos. We are generous and acutely empathic. But our strengths are also our weaknesses: we can be abysmally selfish and greedy. My fellow actors often make me think of Jesus' warning that he doesn't mind the hot and the cold—it's the lukewarm he spits out of his mouth. Actors are *not* lukewarm. We live hard, and we're good at celebration.

My career is often so full of celebration and gifts that it becomes like some continuing Christmas holiday. Christmas holidays, we who celebrate may know, can be very costly and utterly exhausting. Acting is the same. I paid dearly to achieve success in my profession, and now, in the midst of abundance, I try to remind myself to make of these gifts—my life itself being the core gift—something it might please God to receive. When I am acting and employed, or auditioning and unemployed, I try to remind myself that life is good, and what I make of it depends on what I have done, or what I have failed to do.

For the grace of that reminder, I thank my Church—and my Catholic parents and teachers, who formed my conscience according to what they understood and taught as the tenets of their Catholic faith.

Questions for Reflection: *Acting involves wearing different masks and adopting different personas. In what ways does faith challenge us to be true to ourselves, even if we act for a living? How can we best work in an environment in which religious values are not held in great regard? How do you understand the role of your own conscience? What does the Church teach about the role of personal conscience in forming decisions? How do you handle differences of opinion and debates over church teaching in your own life? How does faith encourage or discourage your friendships with colleagues who do not share your faith? Can a strong ego help or hinder faith? How? In what ways can prayer nourish faith? How can faith nourish an overall vision of life as sacred?*

Chapter 12

Hearts Speak to Hearts: On Being a Catholic Artist

Brother Michael O'Neill McGrath, O.S.F.S.

Maybe I romanticize my memories a bit, but it seems to me I loved church when I was a kid. As I recall, I was usually restless and fidgety, bored by all the Latin goings-on, impatient with the demands to be silent, and I absolutely despised getting dressed up in scratchy clothes and having to sit still, but I did savor being in the space where it all occurred. When I walked humbly through the large double doors of a Catholic church, after climbing all those steps, the ordinary suddenly became extraordinary, filling me with a weird mixture of enchantment and the heebie-jeebies. (Is that merely awe, one of those gifts of the Holy Spirit?) The very light was different, colored as it was by the stained glass. The vastness of the space, redolent with beeswax or sometimes incense, swallowed up my tininess. Statues in candlelit niches, paintings and *prie-dieux* in shadowy corners, the priest bellowing, the choir making beautiful, sometimes haunting, music—all of it grabbed me by the senses and touched my soul in ways I could never put into words, then or now.

I sometimes refer to my religious faith as "sexy Catholicism" because of the unique way it has of honoring our human need to touch and be touched. And I don't just mean spiritually touched. I mean flesh-and-bones touched. Blood and hearts, eyes and ears. The stuff that gets artists all riled up with passion and fervor. Catholicism has always loved artists (sometimes in a real love/hate kind of way, to be sure!) because of our unique ability to give flesh to Word and Spirit. Art is a ministry that is played out in a variety of ways: good liturgists and preachers are art-ful as much as potters, weavers, calligraphers, singers, musicians, actors, dancers, poets, and painters, which is where I come in. All of us are just getting up in the morning and looking for a little light in the darkness, a lamp for our feet.

I was afraid of the dark when I was young because I shared a bedroom with two older brothers who loved to scare the hell out of me with stories of horned creatures under the bed or in the closet. Sometimes I would take my pillow and blanket to the hallway, where my mother left a night-light on, and I'd sleep comfortably under the crucifix that hung there. Occasionally I'd stare at it and wait for him to blink or wink at me which, I am happy to report, never happened. Maybe I was just a disturbed child, but I prefer to think I was really latching onto the mystery of the Incarnation through this beautifully carved (and maybe a little creepy) wooden image of God that was a beacon of light in the darkness of my fears. Whichever the case may be, I was discovering that in life as I knew it, art and faith, image and story, all flow like rivers of living water from the same loving source of grace and inspiration.

On the occasional Sunday afternoon, my dad would take us to the Philadelphia Museum of Art, a grand and beautiful building that rests majestically like the Parthenon on the banks of the Schuylkill River. It filled me with awe in the same way church did. Both places were vast and otherworldly, commanding respectful quiet and good behavior. I could no more get too close to a painting or sculpture than I could leap over the altar rail and knock on the tabernacle door. The biggest difference was that the museum had far more naked people on display than did St. Matthew's in northeast Philly.

My favorite single painting to revisit every time was a gigantic Baroque painting by Rubens that showed Prometheus hanging off a ledge, twisted up and upside-down, having his guts pecked out by an eagle. Gooey entrails and naked flesh evoked in me a mixture of fear and fascination, much as God and religion did. All that because the poor guy stole fire from the gods and shared it with the world. Very reminiscent, I thought, of poor Adam and Eve and those troublesome apples filled with knowledge. Perhaps I sensed on some level that the painting was just as much about Rubens as it was about Prometheus because I knew even then that I wanted to be an artist when I grew up. Artists, I learned, were like any other saints and sinners grappling with the big issues of good and evil, only they did it in more interesting ways than most others.

It was the medieval section, however, that really got me going. It was like entering yet another inner world of intrigue and mystery where angels and saints seemed even more real than knights' armor and tapestries. I was fascinated by the mind-boggling attention to detail of gold-gilt carvings and jewel-like paintings. I was excited by the various ways artists would depict familiar stories like St. Francis in ecstasy or St. Agatha and her bloody breasts. My imagination was stirred by the reconstructed cloister garden where I imagined monks and nuns on meditative strolls with paintbrushes in their sleeves, ready to illuminate something at the sound of the next bell. This section of the museum, oddly, felt like home.

I also recall preschool trips downtown with my mother, to Wanamaker's, the famous Philadelphia department store. It was unthinkable to get on the el and head home without first "making a visit" to St. John's Church on 13th Street. Tall and gothic, it was dwarfed by the highrise office buildings of glass and steel that surrounded it. There, my mother would sit still in hushed, blessed silence, momentarily free from kids and worries and home ties that bind. She'd give me a quarter to light a candle (and get me out of her hair?) at the shrine of Our Lady of Lourdes, all done in rocks like the real thing over in France. Mary glowed with candlelight in a cave-like room of inky, velvet shadows. The shrine was hot from flame and covered with gobs of hardened wax. A little spooky, it was an oasis, a heart, a womb, beneath the busy throbs of the street above.

Before climbing the steps to sunlight, we would stop in the bookshop to browse. My mother would look at devotional pamphlets and novenas, while I went for the stories of saints for kids, their pages filled with garish pictures out-coloring any of my favorite comic books. The pictures and stories provided endless entertainment for me—martyrs and missionaries, apostles and virgins (whatever they were). Tales of blood spilt and sacrifices made, moments of pure light in seas of turmoil like grottoes beneath the streets of the city, pulsating and alive. I couldn't wait to get home and draw.

So, art and religious faith go hand in hand for me. I don't recall a time in life when I haven't loved to draw or paint. A bit shy (then) and totally inept at sports (still), art has continuously given me a sense of doing something unique and worthwhile. Only now, with middle-aged eyes, I see it as a sacred calling, a *vocation*, to coin a Catholic school word. Art is prayer and sacrament. There was, however, a gap between boyhood and midlife in which I didn't see it that way.

I spent eleven years as a college art teacher painting very unmemorable landscapes on the side. Occasionally, I'd crank one out which my very harsh inner critic would label as acceptable, but in general I was never pleased. My perfectionism and self-consciousness made it impossible to work with any kind of freedom or ease. I had too wide an array of favorite artists I was trying to emulate. I'd spend weeks on something only to impulsively decide one day to make drastic changes. Day scenes turned into night; clouds came and went in restless abandon; whole seasons changed in the flick of a brush. Artists are supposed to be tormented and restless, are they not? Besides, landscapes were both safe and universally appealing. I was painting to please others, trying to manufacture a life that wasn't really there. This is not what good, productive, and contented artists do. When I see these paintings now, it is as if they were painted by another person. And indeed they were.

It took true tragedy to knock some sense into me. I didn't know what real angst was until each of my parents died when I was in my thirties. Suddenly aware of life's brevity, my longings for affirmation, fame, and success were eventually (painstakingly) supplanted by longings to just live fully and well through the loves of my life, one of which is my work. Pain had taught me a lesson: that I could no longer squander my talents by painting what I *wanted* to be in my heart. I had to look at what was already *really* there, embrace it and express it. It takes too much wasted time and futile energy to try to force the stream any other way!

But tragedy wasn't my only teacher. What I also learned at this time was that I needed to let go of my locked-in, stereotypical notions of what art is and what artists do. Only then could I see how these things connect not only to my life in community as a religious brother but also to business. Can art and spirituality sleep with business and marketing? I didn't used to think so, but I do now. I also began to rethink the urge to make distinctions between art and illustration, between "fine" art and "commercial" art. I stopped judging my work as inferior or superior depending on which of those narrowly defined categories it came from, and decided to just enjoy creating images. I came to believe that it doesn't matter what others think, especially art critics and exhibit judges. What matters is letting the work out of your system, giving birth to a new vision, or better yet, an old and familiar vision presented in a new and personal way.

It was just like that Light that knocked good old St. Paul to the ground and scared the eyesight right out of him. The overwhelming light of the Holy Spirit comes to us in our grief and can leave us temporarily blind and disoriented, but we do eventually pick ourselves up, renewed and ready to face the world again. Once back on my feet with my new set of eyes, I rediscovered all the things that I'd forgotten, things that had been there all along, ever since childhood, beneath those uninspired landscapes that blocked my view. I came to see a world of sacred images and stories, paintings of Jesus, Mary, and saints that first came to me with such power when I slept on the hallway floor when I was four or, later, in church and at the museum. It was all being returned to me, images I'd desired to paint for ages, stories I'd been longing to tell, secret all those years, even to me. I suddenly knew that sacred art was the ministry given to me, the place where I would find my heart's joy.

Painting my favorite saints and stories brought me a newly awakened zeal for my artistry, like a pilgrim heading off to new lands. Determined to never paint another lifeless landscape, I instead conjured up images of Jesus and Mary, or scenes from their lives and age-old devotions to them. Sacred Hearts emerged from my brush alongside Joyful Mysteries,

Black Madonnas, and martyrs old and new. As commissions from publishers and churches came my way, I began to read extensively again the lives of the saints and spiritualities of art. With great enthusiasm, I discovered that I love to take the old and traditional and reconfigure it into something new and fresh. My paintings are my way of saying that traditions and people don't really die, they just change—and that change is good, often painfully so.

I've never been one of those artists who won't speak about his art, who feels the finished piece should speak for itself. In fact, I tend toward the other extreme. You can't shut me up! My experience has always been that the work becomes much more alive to the worshipping community who sees it (and, hopefully, prays with it) when the stories are told and explanations of the symbols are given. We are brought to a deeper level of awareness. This is something I learned teaching art history all those years to college students. I'm always happy to explain why a particular color is chosen or why a particular object is present. God is in the details.

I also think it is sometimes appropriate and beneficial to explain what was going on inside of me, not just what ended up on the painted surface. When I am willing to bare my soul that way, to share my inner vision, as it were, it somehow gives people permission to feel their own hurts and memories, to not feel so alone in the midst of their anxieties.

As St. Francis de Sales said, "Lips speak to ears, only hearts can speak to hearts." Art is healing in that way, the artist a healer-priest.

So, excited to share the stories orally as well, a retreat ministry has evolved in which I use art and story to present new ways of seeing God present in our world. Were those years of painting landscapes a waste of time? Do I regret those hours and hours of restless struggle before blank canvases? Not at all. I wasn't wasting time, I was filling it with lessons and experience. I was learning how to handle paint and ink, how to develop technique and personal style and, most important of all, I was learning how to truly see God in the details of the world. All of it was instrumental in preparing me for the devastation of grief and my St. Paul moment on the road to Damascus. The landscapes before me led me to the world within, a far broader vista with more vivid color.

My restless artist's heart understands what Jesus meant when he said that what we hear in the dark, we must speak in the light. That's what inspiration is all about. Or St. Paul wrote in his letter to the Romans—that if we don't know how to pray, the Holy Spirit will do it for us with groans too deep for words. All of our hearts are groaning always. And it understands, also, what Henri Matisse meant when he said he wanted his paintings to have the same effect on the viewer as does an easy chair after a long day at work. These things are what being an artist means to me—bringing to the light of day the groans of a heart that expresses itself best with symbols, colors, and lines. They emerge from me to touch the weary hearts of others. And in the process, together, we discover grace.

Questions for Reflection: *How do you feel when you enter a church? What appeals to you most: ornate churches with statues of saints, stained glass, and marble altars, or simple churches with sparse design and furnishings? What are your favorite examples of religious art? In what ways has the role of the artist been important to the Church? How might art help you to pray and connect more intimately to God?*

Chapter 13

The Practice of Presence: On Being a Catholic Doctor

David Loxterkamp

I live in a small town. I have had a presence here for seventeen years. Most in my community call me "doctor." Some know me by my religion; others, as a runner or as an occasional writer. Fewer still know me as their friend, their father, or their husband. You might say that I am an amalgam of my relationships.

But these, in turn, converge on an interior terrain, a place inhabited by boyhood memories, the lessons of those who raised and mentored me, the comfort of books, the company of saints. It is a rich and expanding geography, inside and out. Yet, no matter how far my career takes me or how deeply I dive into the realms of the heart, I know that I travel in the sovereignty of faith.

§§ §§ §§

On those reluctant mornings, the alarm clock would rattle me from a flanneled sleep and fling me into the frosty air. Limbs tunneled through sleeves, trod down creaky wooden stairs, parked me behind a cereal box, and pushed me past our front screen door into the lamped and shadowy mysteries of Elm Street, 6:35 A.M.

At the streak of dawn, while the Iowa Plains held its breath, I scurried past the homes of my neighbors: the Biedermans, Bierstedts, Schoenbergers, Schotts. These were families whose lawns I mowed, walks I shoveled, kids I caroused with, lives I intersected as regularly and rightly as the checkerboard streets of my Midwestern home. At Leadley's I would veer left, climb the embankment of the Chicago & Northwestern, take the tracks to the parking lot of the Catholic church—and here behold one of my clearest childhood images, the bricks of St. Margaret's glowing crimson in the angled light.

What survives as a "Catholic sensibility" was born at weekday Mass. In our farming community, the obligation fell to a handful of us "townies." And from a shallow pool were netted young acolytes for the Latin Rite, Benediction,

Stations, Rogations. Here I began to appreciate the liturgy's sobering silence, and to feel the deep satisfaction of doing my part. My physician-father, the local G.P., drove home this point at the supper table: much is expected where much is given.

Silence is not so much the absence of sound but a presence of mind. On my morning walks, the street came alive with cardinals and robins chirping, bread trucks rumbling along the highway, tractors whining from a far-off field. Inside the sacristy, silence was refined by the rustle of starched white surplus over silken cassock, coughs from the crouching widows who prayed in the shadows of the unlit church, and an occasional clunk of a coin dropped in the votive box. The Mass cradled its own ethereal silence, a vaporous refuge where the poetry of the Latin prayers could not anchor me to the *Confetior*, *Agnus Dei*, or the *Orate Fratres* at the close of Offertory: *Suscipiat Dominus sacrificium, de manibus tuis ad laudem et gloriam nominis sui, ad utilitatem quoque nostram, totiusque Ecclesiae suae sanctae.*

In our small farming community, God expressed himself through the customs and constraints of the farming cycle. Seasons were never sentimental. They prescribed our duty to plant in spring, harvest in fall, cultivate in summer, and prepare in the Advent of winter. The lay of the land—flat, unshielded, vast, vacant—set our social expectations. No fence separated us from our neighbor, nor did our doors lock them outside. We shared a single school, grocery store, post office, barber shop; and from within these walls we shared each other's business. The economy hinged on grain yields and market prices. My friends' 4-H projects found their way to the meat locker, and my father was seldom paid until harvest (if at all) in the leaner years when hail, drought, or bottoming farm prices kept the whole community on edge.

One of the altar boy's few rewards was the chance to serve at funerals. Before the church bell began its slow toll, I would race across the playground of Rolfe Consolidated School and suit up for that great ecclesial salvage operation, the Requiem Mass. An added bonus was a trip to the cemetery, which meant another hour away from school and a steaming plate of baked ham, peas, and potato salad from the ladies of the Rosary Society. But my familiarity with holy water and incense, black cope and vestments, the white pall draping the casket on its sturdy bier, could not prepare me for my father's unexpected occupation of the center stage. On that Memorial Day weekend, in my fourteenth year, I remember how the whole town turned out, not only for his funeral but at our front door for weeks on end, bearing covered dishes to fill our emptiness.

In those days of imponderable mystery and loss, I learned that the important things in life happened behind appearances, beyond what could be proven or deposited in a bank. I took solace in the silences, and in my prayers at the bedside where even the All-powerful took time to listen.

௫ ௫ ௫

My wife and I moved halfway across the continent to establish a new home and begin my career. We are now raising two children in whose incredulous hands lie the future of the faith. The house we bought in 1988—known even now as the Percy McGeorge Place—was already a century old. It has been in a state of perpetual repair ever since: new dormers here, bay windows there, and an addition out back, the gulag we call "the playroom." There is a different color and shape and flow to the house than when Percy owned it, but it still stands. It enjoys unbroken use. It provides shelter and security for another generation.

So too have I remodeled the medical practice my father handed down. Though the profession has changed, you can recognize it in the smells of the waiting room, a mix of mud and garlic, ripe diapers and wood smoke. Here mingle mill workers from MBNA and Champion Paper, the bent and the aged, welfare moms and wailing newborns, dairy farmers and lobstermen.

Early on, my partner and I decided that we would string no fences nor lock the door. Our patients would be welcomed regardless of gender, complaint, or ability to pay. Many turned out to be devotees of Chinese acupuncture, chiropractic, homeopathy, reflexology, so it was the family doctor who felt himself the "alternative healer." Not a few of our patients left us for other practices, but since we all shop in the same markets and send our kids to the same schools, none of us doctors can hide from our mistakes.

Gradually I have come to know my patients. This asset I owe to what Catholics call the sacramental nature of the clinical encounter. Inside a fifteen-minute exam, patient and doctor meet for a moment bracketed off the rest of their lives. We may squander the time on finding the right pill or blood test, or filling a form for the insurance carrier. But somehow the doctor establishes his presence and thereby opens the door to grace.

The outward signs of the sacrament are simple: a closed door; the gesture of a handshake and touch of the physical exam; words of welcome and reassurance and acceptance. The doctor, by virtue of his authority and experience, invites the patient to share his suffering. And through the faith, hope, and charity of each participant, the healing arts unfold.

Henri Nouwen once observed that "people expect too much from speaking, too little from silence." How true it is for the doctor, who came prepared to act and decide. But as he listens, the patient's chief complaint transforms itself:

"weight loss" is revealed to be an eating disorder; "migraine" becomes the manifestation of marital discord; a blemish on the skin opens, during its excision, to a blemished past. Secrets are confessed to the innocent bystander—poor substitute that I am for the therapist or parish priest.

My Catholic upbringing serves me well. Through the rituals of medicine, I help patients face their addiction, moral weakness, or impending death. Not uncommonly, the diagnosis or an admission to the hospital will lead them to a sudden insight or act of forgiveness. The Church has sharpened my edges for paring away uncertainty, conflict, and disabling doubt, but restrains me with a reminder that my true authority flows from a merciful God.

In my work, the markers of progress are less and less a lowered cholesterol level or well-organized chart, a clearing chest X-ray or resolving rash. They have come to be the immeasurable yet doubtless gains of hope in the provence of despair. For the physician-scientist, there are neurochemicals to account for. For the public health official, there are bare essentials like food and shelter that are required for one's well-being. There are achievements by which the contented, reading only the labels of material success, judge the relative happiness of others. But the doctor and patient who arrive in others' presence will speak of a happiness that comes from knowing what is essential in life and relinquishing all else.

၆ ၆ ၆

Outside the office, I have found a second home in Hospice. For among the dying there is no time for illusion or excuse: the clock is ticking and all we can do is wait. The doctor waits, too, in a chair set beside the family, resting perhaps for the first time that day. Here I unravel my vestments, tuck away the stethoscope and prescription pad, and forego the little talk I often give to shore up my treatments or buffer myself against intimacy. Instead, I speak of my own losses and fears, the deaths of my parents, my children at risk. I might mention the morning I spent with Bonnie and her dying husband. It was a Monday, I recall. Despite all the encouraging news from the cancer specialists, we watched as the gleam in his eyes clouded over. The tidal breathing finally flattened to a nod of his chin, then ceased. We spoke of their courtship, their life together before and after the move to Maine, her feelings of rejection, his worries about money. When I finally mentioned her husband's death—had she noticed? Bonnie nodded.

"I was afraid to say anything because you would have pronounced him dead. I suppose it sounds foolish, but I thought if we kept talking he would never leave us."

In another room across town, I visited a family whose matriarch lay in a coma. Family members whom I have treated for years but never associated with Mrs. M. poked their familiar heads from around wallpapered edges and shadowy corners of the tiny apartment. The air was so thick with cigarette smoke that I was tempted to list "asphyxiation" as the principle cause of death. They didn't ask me to save their mother, or even require that I pronounce her dead. All they needed was a doctor to certify that "everything medical" had been done, and that the children had been dutiful in their expected roles.

In my weekly house calls to a patient dying of cancer, I struggle with my own crisis of faith. How can a person kindle hope when his or her world shrinks to a queen-sized bed, where the only variations are in the degree of pain or strength of odor from a bedsore? Together we battle against discouragement, and his or her fear that the next breath will be the last.

Yes, you say, faith is quiet comfort for the doctor who ponders his practice at the close of the day, or sizes up his career when nothing more can be said or done. But what does it hold for the board-certified physician working at full stride? I put this question to my colleagues at a recent convention. Can the unhappy doctor practice good medicine? Can a technically proficient specialist fail in his obligations? Can we justify our fees when the waiting room is full of patients who suffer self-limited disease, excessive worry, the ravages of age, acts of self-abuse, abject poverty, boredom, or terminal disease? What is it we actually offer them?

I described my acquaintance with a dairy farmer, Beaver Simmons, and his several hundred-acre farm atop Morey Hill near my home in Maine. Spoke of his commitment to his herd, but also to his neighbors and the rules of husbandry that guide his labors. Our friendship has become a multi-spoked wheel that unites our faith, my rural past, a widening circle of friends, and the age-old agrarian ideals that were bred in my Iowan bones—the value of staying put and keeping connected. His dairy operation parallels my own practice; both deal in units of production—the lactating cow, the diseased patient who can be treated as a commodity and revenue line. Or appreciated in a richer sense for their companionship, individuality, grace under adversity, and God-given purpose on earth.

There is always a question for the doctor beyond the technical problem he has been trained to solve. Pain, for example, can be quantified on a ten-point scale and treated with a morphine pump. But a patient's suffering lies in the spiritual domain. Thus are we drawn outside the *terra firma* of our training—far from reason, empiricism, and the undisputed facts. Family doctors tread on ice flows of faith. We leap open water with our bag of tricks in pursuit of the illusory and shifting needs of our patients. Without faith, how can it be done? Forget religion. Speak only of confidence in ourselves, our profession, and the worthiness of our patients. Define it, like my dear stepmother does, as something "I can't prove but I know it's true."

Everyday I struggle to be more than the self-important doctor whose own agenda prevents him from knowing and loving his patients and seeing his own reflection in their sorrow. I have suffered lapses of a technical as well as moral nature, only to discover that my patients have already forgiven me and preferred the error come at my hand over any other. And despite my rush to judgment about their stupidity or self-destructiveness, rudeness or ingratitude, I blush to discover—in their presence—that our relationship has made a difference.

ဪ ဪ ဪ

I do not think of myself as "Catholic" any more than in an ordinary day I would call myself a "Mainer" or a "family man." Religion is a thread in the general fabric; it is the exterior hide we inhabit.

But there are days—after returning from a family vacation or a medical meeting—when I become aware of what sustains me. I listen to our prayers at the supper table. I glance at the poster of St. Dominic bent in *lectio divina* over my computer, the crucifix beside it that balanced briefly on my father's coffin, the golden scallop shell that symbolizes my quest for God that is and always will be a pilgrimage. Then words in a conversation lance me, words as benevolent as *sacrament, grace, blessing, mystery, mercy*. When I return to church on Sunday I join my neighbors who take their faith seriously, who simultaneously reinforce and test my beliefs. We have come to hear the Word, honor the saints, and celebrate the Sacrifice and community that is the Mass. We have come for the presence.

Every other Sunday I sing with a folk group called the Wildflowers. We steal our name from a ragamuffin ensemble Annie Dillard described in her essay "An Expedition to the Pole." With our untrained voices, stuttering starts, and occasional (col)lapses of memory, we make a joyful clamor unto the Lord. But here you will find us, in faithful return to the sanctuary of our chapel. I am the family doctor for half the group. In my dual capacity I have both cared for and disappointed them. We are simply Catholics struggling with our imperfections in the lee of God's grace.

Much of my life is ruled by clinical guidelines, codes conduct, and the laws of human biology. This is no excuse, only a setting, as Father Nouwen reassures us: "Even the cenobite [monk] knew that his Rule was only an exterior framework, a kind of scaffolding with which he was to help himself build the spiritual structure of his own life. . . . There was nothing to which they had to 'conform' except the secret, hidden, inscrutable will of God . . ." The will of God is not an easy path nor a message set in stone. It springs from that inexhaustible source I once tapped in my bedside petitions and now praise in Sunday song. It is the Will of all gentleness and love.

At long last I am catching on to his plan. I see how it is advanced through the agency of my patients, my family, and the testing ground called community. I cherish the rewards he has planted for me within the traditions of the Church. Counted among these are the gift of my vocation, a belief that the doctor is—without apology—a servant of the sick, and the certainty that I give in gratitude for all that I've been given.

Questions for Reflection: *Doctors encounter human beings at all stages of life, from birth to death. Can you think of some of the lessons about life that doctors might receive from patients? In what ways is practicing medicine a ministry? How can faith help doctors in their practice? How might illness enable a person to draw closer to God? Doctors often describe the importance of being physically present to patients. What is a ministry of presence?*

About the Contributors

Ron Hansen grew up in Omaha, Nebraska, where he was educated by Dominican nuns at Holy Angels Grade School, and by Jesuits at Creighton Preparatory School and Creighton University. He earned an M.F.A. in fiction writing at the University of Iowa's Writers Workshop, was a Wallace Stegner Creative Fellow at Stanford, and received an M.A. in spirituality from Santa Clara University, where he is now the Gerard Manley Hopkins, S.J., Professor in the Arts and Humanities. He is the author of *Nebraska*, a collection of stories, of the novels *Hitler's Niece*, *Atticus*, *Mariette in Ecstasy*, *The Assassination of Jesse James by the Coward Robert Ford*, and *Desperadoes*, and of *A Stay Against Confusion: Essays on Faith and Fiction*. He is married to the writer Bo Caldwell and lives in northern California.

Lucie J. Fjeldstad has over thirty-five years experience in the development and marketing of information products. She has been credited by both industry and the national press as a visionary and a pioneer in shaping the convergence of the video, computing, telecommunications, media/entertainment, and consumer electronics industries into a concept referred to as the "information highway." Lucie Fjeldstad was most recently the CEO and president of DataChannel, Inc., and has been the CEO and president of Fjeldstad International; corporate vice president and president of the Video and Networking Division at Tektronix, Inc.; and for twenty-five years worked with IBM in many capacities from programming to a corporate vice president position. Lucie Fjeldstad currently sits on the board of directors for Adaptec, Inc., and has served on the board of regents for Santa Clara University and the board of trustees for Carnegie Mellon University, Syracuse University, and the UCLA Foundation. She holds a bachelor's degree in economics from Santa Clara University and a master's degree in economics from the University of California, Los Angeles (UCLA). She and her husband make their home in Kirkland, Washington.

David H. Armitage is the Director of Design and Construction at the Planning Office for Urban Affairs, the housing development office of the Archdiocese of Boston. A registered architect, David has been involved in the creation of buildings for over twenty years. He is a graduate of St. John's University, Collegeville, Minnesota, the Boston Architectural Center, and the University of Cambridge, England. He and his partner, Philip, live in Boston.

John A. Eterno has served in the New York City Police Department for almost twenty years, where he is currently captain in the Mapping Support Unit. After earning his doctorate in criminal justice, Dr. Eterno published his research on diverse aspects of law enforcement—training, corruption, drug screening of suspects, zero-tolerance policing. He is happily married to his wife JoAnn and has a baby daughter, Julia Marie, who was born on December 24, 2001.

Amelia J. Uelmen graduated from Georgetown University Law Center in 1993. She wrote this essay while working in the litigation department of the New York office of a large law firm. She is currently the director of Fordham University Law School's Institute on Religion, Law & Lawyer's Work, which is developing resources and programs to help practicing lawyers and law students in their efforts to live integrated lives of faith in the context of the challenges of today's legal practice and law school environment.

Terry Golway has been a journalist for nearly thirty years and is currently city editor and columnist for the *New York Observer*, as well as a columnist for the Jesuit weekly magazine *America*. He is also the author of five books, including *Full of Grace*, an oral biography of Cardinal John O'Connor, and a forthcoming history of the Fire Department of New York, entitled *That Others Might Live*. He lives with his wife,

Eileen, and their children, Kate and Conor, in Maplewood, New Jersey.

Sidney Callahan, Ph.D., is a psychologist, Catholic ethicist, and writer on religious and moral questions. She is the author of countless essays and several books, including *In Good Conscience: Reason and Emotion in Moral Decision Making.* Sidney and her husband have been married for forty-seven years; they live in Ardsley-on-Hudson, New York, and have six grown children and four grandchildren.

Paul Mariani taught English literature, with an emphasis on twentieth-century poetry, at the University of Massachusetts, Amherst, for thirty-two years. After he retired he accepted a chair in English at Boston College, where he presently teaches. He has published fourteen books, including five books of poetry, four biographies (of William Carlos Williams, John Berryman, Robert Lowell, and Hart Crane), critical studies of Gerard Manley Hopkins and William Carlos Williams, two books of critical essays, a spiritual autobiography called *Thirty Days: On Retreat with the Exercises of St. Ignatius* (Viking Putnam), and a book of essays called *God and the Imagination: On Poets, Poetry, and the Ineffable* (University of Georgia Press). He lives with his wife, Eileen, in Montague, Massachusetts.

Monica Kolb Andrews graduated from Creighton University, Omaha, Nebraska, in 1994 with a degree in environmental sciences. At Creighton she was active in a variety of service activities, including a service learning semester abroad in the Dominican Republic. After graduation she returned to Latin America and worked with the *Rostro de Cristo* Mission Volunteer Program in Duran, Ecuador, for sixteen months, and then in the summer of 1996 returned to the Dominican Republic as a site coordinator with Creighton's Institute for Latin American Concern. She earned a master's degree in social services and a master's degree in law and social policy from Bryn Mawr College, Bryn Mawr, Pennsylvania, in 2000, and currently works in the Cystic Fibrosis Center at a children's hospital in Philadelphia. She lives with her husband, Michael, in Havertown, Pennsylvania.

Tom McGrath is the author of *At Home with our Faith*, the family spirituality newsletter from Claretian Publications, and *Raising Faith-Filled Kids: Ordinary Opportunities to Nurture Spirituality at Home* (Loyola Press). He enjoys life in Chicago with his wife and two college-age daughters. Tom is a frequent retreat leader and presenter on family life as a spiritual path, and a content-provider for the family website www.homefaith.com.

Mimi Kennedy is a working actress who lives in Los Angeles with her husband and two teenage children. After twelve years of Catholic education and attending Smith College in Northampton, Massachusetts, she began acting in theater, films, and television. She has played Abby, Dharma's hippie mother, on the sitcom *Dharma and Greg* since 1997. She is also author of *Taken to the Stage; The Education of an Actress* (Smith and Kraus, 1996).

Michael O'Neill McGrath, O.S.F.S., a religious brother in the Oblates of St. Francis de Sales, is an internationally recognized artist. His work has been commissioned for churches, organizations, and individuals, and has been featured in both the religious and the secular media. He has published several books of his art and writing on the saints, including *Journey with Thérèse of Lisieux: Celebrating the Artist in Us All* (Sheed & Ward, 2001). In addition to creating artwork, Brother Mickey works nationally as a speaker and director of retreats, workshops, and parish missions, dealing with the healing power of art and its relationship to prayer. He lives in Washington, D.C.

David Loxterkamp is a family doctor from Belfast, a working-class community on the coast of Maine. With his wife Lindsay McGuire, they are raising two children, Clare and John. Dr. Loxterkamp describes himself as a runner, an aficionado of architecture, and an occasional writer. He is the author of *A Measure of My Days: The Journal of a Country Doctor* (University Press of New England, 1997).

About the Editors

James Martin, S.J., is Associate Editor of *America* Magazine and author of, most recently, *In Good Company: The Fast Track from the Corporate World to Poverty, Chastity, and Obedience* (Sheed & Ward, 2000). Winner of three Catholic Press Association awards for his articles and books, he is author of *This Our Exile* (Orbis, 1999) and editor of *How Can I Find God?* (Liguori, 1997).

Jeremy Langford is the Co-publisher/Editor-in-Chief of Sheed & Ward and author of *God Moments: Why Faith Really Matters to a New Generation* (Orbis, 2001). Editor of Cardinal Joseph Bernardin's best-selling memoir *The Gift of Peace* (Loyola, 1997), Langford has published numerous articles and is contributing author to *Happy Are They* (Triumph Books, 1997), and co-editor of *The Journey to Peace* (Doubleday, 2001).